HOW TO WRITE HORROR FICTION

HOW TO WRITE HORROR FICTION

WILLIAM F. NOLAN

Writer's
Digest
Books

Cincinnati, Ohio

95   94   93   5   4   3   2

**Library of Congress Cataloging-in-Publica-
tion Data**

Nolan, William F.
   How to write horror fiction / by William F.
Nolan.
      p.   cm.
   Includes bibliographical references and in-
dex.
   ISBN 0-89879-442-0 (hard cover : alk. pa-
per)
   1. Horror tales—Authorship. 2. Fantastic
literature—Authorship.
I. Title.
PN3377.5.H67N65   1990   90-12911
808.3'8738—dc20   CIP

The following page is an extension of this
copyright page.

Permissions Acknowledgments

Acknowledgments

I wish to thank Nancy Dibble, my editor at Writer's Digest Books, as well as Barbara Puechner, my agent, for making this book happen. I am also grateful to J. N. Williamson for his cooperation and friendship.

My wife, Cam, is due special thanks for her loving support and expert work on the manuscript.

Finally, I honor the memory of three remarkable individuals who were strongly influential in my life and career within the genre of dark fantasy: Charles Beaumont, Rod Serling, and Boris Karloff. Without them, this book would never have been written.

William F. Nolan
Reseda, California

For my horrific friend,

J. N. Williamson

Cheers, Jerry!

Contents

The essential element [of horror] is the clash between prosaic everyday life and a mysterious, irrational, and potentially supernatural universe.
          —Douglas E. Winter

We make up horrors to help us cope with the real ones.
          —Stephen King

Introduction

With *How to Write Horror Fiction*, my intention is simple. I intend to make this book a very personal one; I will, in effect, be talking on paper. My subject will be horror in all its varied forms and aspects: its roots and history, how it is achieved, who writes it and why, the elements that shape it, and the directions it is taking in today's computer age.

My aim will be to demonstrate how you can generate, write, and sell your own work in this fascinating genre. I'll be talking to you about what I have experienced, profited by, and absorbed in more than three decades of professional writing. I shall be quoting from my published work to demonstrate my points. My personal history in the genre of fright will serve as a road map, outlining the route you will need to follow if you wish to reach your goal.

The first time I stood on a public stage to deliver a lecture, I was a nervous wreck; the palms of my hands were sweating and I could barely catch my breath. I could feel my heart hammering in my chest.

All this anxiety was self-created. I had allowed the word *lecture* to intimidate me. Once I began to speak, I realized that the way to communicate was not to *lecture* my audience, in a dry, academic sense, but to *talk* to them, as if they had gathered in my living room to hear a story. Having made this discovery, I immediately relaxed. I wanted to tell them some things that they were there to hear; we became a single organism, my mind linked to all the minds in the room.

That's the same approach I will be using in this book. I want you to imagine that we're in a room together, comfortable, relaxed, with no pressure on either of us. Just you and me, with this book as our mind-link. I'll be talking to you in these pages about the subject of horror, with the idea of exciting you to its possibilities, of sparking your imagination, of demonstrating the methods and techniques that will enable you to exert your own individual creativity within this genre.

So sit back—and let's talk.

I have a lot to tell you.

W.F.N.

1.
EXPLORING THE DARK SIDE

Fear is fun. Being frightened is delicious. We tend to giggle when we're really scared—partly to expel the tension, partly because we're having such a good time. I'm not talking *real* fear. No one enjoys encountering a knife at the throat, or facing a loaded gun, or fighting the horrors of cancer or AIDS. But a book or a movie or a TV show can't physically hurt us. Instead, they provide an escape hatch, a way for us to deal with the fact that death is as natural as birth and that no one gets out of life alive. Manufactured horror on a page, in a theater, or on a television screen, allows us to transcend our own mortality—at least for the duration of the story. It's a way to surmount the horrors of the real world. And, as I say, it's a lot of fun. That's why we allow ourselves to be frightened over and over. By tapping into our primal fears, bringing the things of darkness into the light, we achieve an act of personal triumph. We feel brave; we've faced the monster and *survived*. We emerge with a grin and a giggle; we've put Old Mr. Death in his place.

It's really that basic. That's the root of it all, this constant fright game played by all of us, writers and readers and moviegoers. Of course, there are many complex levels to this basic act of self-created fear, and I'll be getting into them in due course.

Right now, I want to talk about how it began, back there in the ancient days before Rod Serling invited us all to enter the twilight zone. I'm going to make this personal. I'll start in the 1940s, then do some time jumping back into the actual history of the genre.

Let's begin with the summer of 1943. In Kansas City, Missouri. Hot and muggy. I'm fifteen, and school's out until the fall. I can bike down to the library, or walk to the drugstore for a malt and the latest superhero comic, or take in a movie. Or I can go to a bookstore.

I do that. I walk into this bookstore to check out what's new. I love to read. I've got my allowance, so I have enough to buy a Tower book. They're published in hardcover. The country's at war, so they use cheap paper; it quickly turns yellow at the edges like old parchment. But the good part is Tower books cost just fifty cents.

One jumps out at me. Not literally, but it *feels* as if it's been put there just for me. Boris Karloff's head is on the front jacket, below a pair of staring eyes and a shadowy hand. Already, I love horror movies, and Karloff is my favorite actor—the Frankenstein monster himself. And here he is, on a book titled *Tales of Terror*.

"The world's most terrifying stories presented by the outstanding living exponent of horror." Wow! This one has to be a winner.

I dig out my fifty cents and take the book home. Then I hunker down in the shade of the back porch and begin reading Mr. Karloff's selections.

The titles alone are enough to give any kid the shivers: "The Waxwork" . . . "Clay-Shuttered Doors" . . . "The Damned Thing" . . . "The Hound" . . . "The Tell-Tale Heart" . . . "The Beast With Five Fingers" . . . and my favorite of the lot, "The Willows." (It was written by a fellow I'd never heard of, Algernon Blackwood, which I thought was a great name for a horror writer.)

Here, in one book, was Poe and Bram Stoker (the horrific pleasures of his novel, *Dracula*, were still in my future) and Joseph Conrad and William Faulkner and Ambrose Bierce. I'd lucked out. Old Boris had taken me by the hand and led me into the wondrous world of printed terror. My first full excursion into the genre left me breathless.

A lifelong addiction had been activated.

I began to read horror as avidly as I watched it on the screen. In 1944, two other classic anthologies entered my life: *Sleep No More*, edited by August Derleth, and *Great Tales of Terror and the Supernatural*, edited by Herbert Wise and Phyllis Fraser. (The latter book is still in print, and no real horror buff should be without a copy.)

I read my first Robert Bloch story in the Derleth book, and was introduced to John Collier and the legendary H.P. Lovecraft (with his classic of grue, "The Rats in the Walls"). In *Great Tales of Terror and the Supernatural*, I encountered the work of Henry James, A.E. Coppard, Arthur Machen, and a host of others, including W.W. Jacobs with his back-from-the-dead masterwork, "The Monkey's Paw."

I was faithfully buying each garishly illustrated monthly issue of *Weird Tales* (from whose pages Ray Bradbury exploded into my life with "The Jar"), and was soon sniffing out other anthologies of horror at the library and from local Kansas City bookshops with the zeal and dedication of a beagle on the hunt. The history of this form of literature didn't concern me in those days; I just wanted to experience the chills of a dark new world of ghosts, demons, vampires, and assorted creatures of the night.

The Humanness of Fear

Horror, in one form or another, has been with us since the dawn of civilization. The human animal has been, by nature, uncertain and apprehensive; we are in awe of a universe too vast for us to comprehend. Superstition and a fear of the unknown have dominated humankind. We've based our cultures on an abiding belief in the supernatural, in powers beyond this known world, whether we view them as demonic or angelic.

Entire populations have structured their ways of life on the casting of bones, the reading of entrails or tea leaves. Both men and women have been burned at the stake for witchcraft, and the treasures of a person's life have been buried with the corpse to ensure that a troubled spirit would not return to haunt the living.

Today, we can scoff at these things — but the residual fears are still there. Would you really be willing to spend the night in a "haunted" graveyard, or sleep in a room where multiple murders were committed? Maybe. But you'd be damned nervous doing it. After all, something could *be* there in the darkness . . . waiting for you . . .

The dark has always generated tales of terror. Cave dwellers, squatting at their campfires, would exchange stories of fearsome creatures stalking the shadows, and it was a matter of inevitable progression that writers from Edgar Allan Poe to Stephen King should spin out dread tales designed to quicken the heart and challenge the imagination.

Horror is, therefore, a natural part of our human heritage. It partakes of our deepest selves, illuminating the dark side in all of us, the subbasement of the soul.

Horror's Gruesome Beginnings

In 1764, Horace Walpole, an English nobleman (who later became the fourth Earl of Oxford and who sat in Parliament for twenty-six years) authored a medieval novel set in a haunted Italian castle, replete with ghosts in clanking armor, terrified maidens, and spectral apparitions. This was *The Castle of Otranto*, a book that directly influenced Ann Radcliffe's *The Mysteries of Udolpho* (1794), now considered to be the keystone novel in Gothic horror. Mrs. Radcliffe used nearly all of Walpole's haunted castle effects, but with far greater impact and literacy.

However, it took the dark (some say demented) genius of Edgar Allan Poe — with his *Tales of the Grotesque and Arabesque*, published in 1839 — to define the horror story in fully realized terms. Poe gave us classic upon classic, stories etched in the collective consciousness of us all, from "The Tell-Tale Heart" to "Masque of the Red Death," from "The Pit and the Pendulum" to "The Fall of the House of Usher."

Other early masters, such as Robert Louis Stevenson, J. Sheridan Le Fanu, H.G. Wells, and Franz Kafka, carried on from Poe and solidly established the horror story as a significant part of our literary culture.

Fright in Our Times

Throughout the twentieth century, a wide variety of writers extended and broadened the genre. Among them: Robert Aickman, Truman Capote, Fritz Leiber, Jack Finney, Roald Dahl, Shirley Jackson, Jorge Luis Borges, and Nigel Kneale.

In recent years, spearheaded by the immense global popularity of Stephen King, the field of horror has achieved major status as mass-market entertainment. Whenever a new book by King or Dean Koontz or Clive Barker or Peter Straub is published, it becomes an automatic best seller.

On-screen horror seems to be holding its own against the spectacular action-adventure films of Spielberg and Lucas. In fact, since the late 1960s, printed and cinematic horrors have risen in tandem. And when that gruesome little alien critter ate its way out of a crewman's chest in *Alien* in 1979, a new wave of science fiction horror was upon us. From the gory "splatter" school of the *Friday the 13th* series and the films of Clive Barker, to the more civilized terrors of *The Abyss*, and *Batman* (oh, yes, *Batman* is most definitely a fright film), the genre has continued to grow in terms of high profits and mass popularity.

The modern trend in printed horror did not begin with Stephen King. It can be traced to a trio of novels that revitalized the old traditions and opened the doors to bestsellerdom.

The first was *Rosemary's Baby*, by Ira Levin, published in 1967, in which a cult of devil worshipers in a New York apartment house seduce a young housewife into giving birth to the Devil's son. When Roman Polanski directed the motion picture version in 1968, Levin's success was assured; the film was a major hit.

Next, William Peter Blatty's *The Exorcist* soared to the top of the bestseller lists and became a gigantic film success in 1973. Also: Thomas Tryon's *The Other*, published the same year as the *The Exorcist* (1971), became a solid best seller, further elevating the genre to mass-market level.

The stage was set for Stephen King's first horror novel, *Carrie*, published in 1974 and brought to the screen in 1976. A new era in horror had been launched.

Today, in books, in television, and on the motion picture screen, horror is big business around the world. Publishers and industry producers are actively seeking fresh stories in this constantly expanding market, and new writers are entering the field each month. There's no reason, given talent and hard work, that you can't be one of them.

2.
TAKE ME TO YOUR MONSTER

In this chapter, I'm going to talk about monsters. That's because the monster is primary within the field of horror, just as the gunfighter is primary in the Western, or the private eye is primary in hard-boiled detective fiction.

Of course, you *can* write horror without writing about monsters — but even when no particular monster is present, there must be something *monstrous* inherent in the body of your story or novel.

In James Kisner's shock tale, "The Litter," those wiggling things born of his cat and the neighbor's dog are certainly not kittens or puppies. They are a mutant form of life, fanged and instantly dangerous, and they immediately devour the animals that served as their entry into our world. As Kisner describes them:

> *. . . not one of them had any fur [and] they had no tails, but they did have claws . . . they looked like ugly hairless moles . . . caked with crusty blood.* Mutations, *I thought;* slimy little bastards.

The monster in the Dean Koontz best seller *The Bad Place* is a savage character with the power to read the minds of his victims and then teleport himself to their homes and offices, where he proceeds to rip out their throats, drink their blood, then kill them. A genuine New Age monster with paranormal talents.

The monster in Ray Bradbury's "The One Who Waits" is an alien well on another planet. Once you've fallen into it, the well claims your soul. In Bradbury's "The Women," it's the sea itself that lures its victims to a watery death.

In J.N. Williamson's deeply moving story, "The House of Life," his monster is an atomic holocaust—and in George R.R. Martin's disturbing novelette, "Sandkings," his protagonist faces malevolent insects who increase in size and ferocity.

In Charles L. Grant's *Bloodwind*, the monster is a killer wind—and the monster in Robert Melville's *Deathday* is a deadly amulet.

Thus, the term embraces almost any type of weird menace, not just the more familiar monsters we all know and love: vampires, ghosts, demons, werewolves, and zombies.

Within the all-expansive genre of horror, you are free to create your own individual monsters who may or may not be supernatural.

In the film *Alien* (and its sequel), the creatures were discovered on another planet. A mix of giant spider (always a popular monster; see *The Incredible Shrinking Man*) and The Gill Man from *The Creature from the Black Lagoon*, they were capable of sucking the life out of the story's human characters.

In John Cheever's "Torch Song," the monster is an outwardly ordinary woman named Joan Harris, who just happens to inflict sickness and death as a by-product of her love—definitely someone to avoid at your neighborhood house party.

What I'm demonstrating here, with these diverse examples, is that your options are wide open as to the type of monster you may wish to create.

Old Ghoul, New Approach

Suppose you have a strong desire to use a ghost or a vampire or a werewolf as your central menace. Is it still possible to utilize such conventional monsters in today's horror fiction? Will editors buy yet another vampire novel when so many have already been written?

The answer is yes: Editors are always receptive to novels and stories containing supernatural monsters, but they must be freshly presented; your stories must offer new insights and a fresh approach.

Stephen King did it with *'Salem's Lot*. He gave us creatures who bloodsucked their way through an entire town in Maine, creating new fellow-vampires with each fanged feast. Anne Rice did it with her bestselling series *Interview With the Vampire*, *The Vampire Lestat*, and *The Queen of the Damned*.

She gave us vampires with fully dimensional backgrounds, and she invested these monsters with levels of human understanding that allowed readers to empathize with them even as they were being shocked and frightened. A fresh, exciting variant.

New vampire novels continue to appear in bookstores every season—proving that there's still plenty of life in the old Undead.

The same holds true for ghosts and werewolves.

Thomas Tessier's *The Nightwalker* is a perfect example of how to achieve freshness and impact in writing about a werewolf. He invests his main character, Bobby Ives, who suffers from this horrific malady, with humanity and depth of character. He allows us to share his mind and inner fears, his uncertainty as to what he is becoming:

> *And then he noticed his hands again—the palms rough, as if edged with tiny beard bristles, the backs hard as horn. A charge roared through every particle of his being, but his fingers seemed to have lost their mobility. They were stiff and crooked, and the hands were dark, dark from more than the dirt they had just held. Ives attempted to push his sleeves back but found the movement difficult. He had to slide his clumsy fingers under the fabric of coat, sweater and shirt, and then pull them back. As he did so his nails raked sharply along leathery flesh. . . . The nails, like razors, actually tore the shirt and sweater.* What is happening to me?

If your monster is indeed supernatural, it is your job to make the creature real and understandable on human terms, despite his supernatural powers. The monster cannot simply rage around the countryside devouring townsfolk like McDonald's Big Macs. You must create a creature readers will believe is *real*. They may be repelled by your monster, but they will follow its adventures once the creature's *reality* has been established.

As I have already pointed out, this reality need not stem from a human base. In his story "The Derelict," William Hope Hodgson presents a ship of living tissue, a deadly fungus that can ensnare and absorb anyone who steps upon its deck. Hodgson created a dread sense of immediate, three-dimensional reality that allowed the reader to suspend disbelief and enter his special world. He accomplished it with careful attention to mood-detail and atmosphere. (I'll be covering mood in a later chapter.)

Always remember, your readers want to go along with you as you take them on your imaginary journey into terror; they want you to convince them, if only for the duration of your story, that such things can be. They are actively seeking the kind of tale you wish to tell.

They'll stick with you all the way, and relish the trip, if you give them a monster with dimension and depth. They don't care about the *form* of your monster—but they demand that you make that monster *real*.

Multiple Monsters

Sometimes you can create two monsters within the same narrative, as I did in my story "The Partnership." My first-person storyteller, Tad Miller, is totally human, with no special powers whatever, but he works with Ed, a thing who lives at the bottom of a lake near a deserted amusement park. Together they form a bizarre partnership. Miller lures a victim to the park, then feeds him to Ed, collecting the victim's wallet, rings, wristwatch, etc., while Ed makes a hearty meal of him.

I make Ed real by describing him through the eyes of his human partner:

> *Ed wasn't much to look at. Kind of weird, really. His father was one of those big rats that live in the burrows under the cemetery, and his mother was something from deep in the lake. Something big and ugly and leathery.*

Later, Miller describes Ed after one of his flesh feasts:

> *His jaw was dripping and his slanted black eyes glittered. Ed never blinked. He was watching me the way he always does, with his tail kind of moving, snakelike. He looked kind of twitchy, so I hurried. I don't think Ed likes the rain. Ed makes me nervous when it rains. He's not himself. I never hang around [the park] when he's like that.*

The ultimate monster-human partnership is, of course, Stevenson's *Dr. Jekyll and Mr. Hyde*—in which we have both good and evil contained in the same body.

I applied another variant of this two-in-one theme in my story "The Francis File," in which the main character is a serial killer so full of self-revulsion that he commits suicide at the climax by entering a demon's blood pentagram and being ripped apart by this other evil entity.

At this point, you may be asking: How many monsters can be included in a single novel or story? If one is scary, or two, then wouldn't six or seven be even scarier?

Peter Straub included several forms of menace in his novel *Floating Dragon* (including a killer gas that literally *melted* several of his characters) — but unless you possess the experience and superior writing skills of a Peter Straub, you'd be wise to limit your monsters to no more than two per story. Even then, one of them should be *central* to your narrative, the other kept in a background or subsidiary position (as my lake thing is in "The Partnership").

Stick in too many monsters and you lose credibility with your readers. Concentrate your attention on one major menace that provides a solid threat to your characters. And don't mix your monsters. A reader may go along with you if you present a realistic werewolf, but if you toss a vampire into the same story, or a ghost, or a zombie, your entire house of reality will collapse around your ears; you will be stretching the reader's willingness to believe well beyond the limit.

And remember, once you've lost your readers, you don't get them back; they will go on to another author who gives them a sense of reality. (I'll be talking a lot more about reality in my discussion of protagonists in Chapter Four.)

Timing for Terror

In a story or novel, when should your monster be introduced? Should you have him, her, or it attack your protagonist in the beginning, perhaps on the opening page?

There is no set rule as to how soon you should bring your monster center-stage front, but in nearly all of the best horror fiction, an *aura* of menace and potential danger is established right away (often in the first paragraph); the monster itself is not introduced until much later, allowing you to provide tension and suspense for your readers as they nervously await meeting your menace at full force. The *actions* of the monster can and should be dramatized early; a murder, or a scene during which the *effect* of the monster is shown without a full revelation of the creature itself.

You'll see how I handled this in my chapter "A Dip in 'The Pool.'" The point is to build reader expectation by a slow process so that when your monster does appear, the groundwork of fear will have been fully laid.

In a short story, that might not be until the climax; in a novel, you can present the monster much earlier, but its *full* powers must not be employed against your protagonist until the climax of the book.

Note how Stephen King handles the buildup of suspense in *The Shining*; his characters don't arrive at the Overlook Hotel, where the real terror begins, until the book is well underway.

And in King's *The Dark Half*, we don't actually meet George Stark until his presence and power have been fully explored for the reader.

Also, the *nature* of your monster should be revealed gradually. We don't want to learn everything there is to know about the creature's powers, intentions, or background too early in the story. It's best to allow the reader to learn about the menace along with your main characters. Sherlock Holmes *gradually* learns about the killer canine in *The Hound of the Baskervilles*. And he does not go out to confront the beast until the book's climax on the moors.

Revealing too much too quickly robs the story of its essential suspense. By withholding facts about the exact nature and full powers of your monster, you keep its threat immediate and fresh throughout the story. And by placing the confrontation between your monster and your protagonist at the end, in the climax, you maintain the monster's fright level to the last page.

The Dominion of Darkness

Just how powerful should your monster be? Should it possess *numerous* powers?

In *The Dark Place*, the monster, known as Candy (and I'll talk about the importance of character names in Chapter Four), has the power to instantly teleport himself out of danger; he is also able to enter the minds of his victims. Also, at will, he can with a pointing finger loose a ball of fire and destruction.

With this character, Koontz has actually crossed the monster line, in my opinion. Candy has been given too many powers. He is, in fact, so powerful that the hero cannot kill him (Candy is destroyed by his also-powerful brother). The protagonist (although he *plans* the action) is a bystander. Koontz breaks many of the rules here—but he had more than fifty novels published before creating this particular monster, so he's entitled to his tour de force.

Ideally, your monster should possess limited powers; it should not be so powerful that the reader feels your hero has no chance to defeat it. And if, by a fluke, your all-powerful monster *is* defeated at the end of the story by your human hero, the readers will not buy your ending. It will seem forced and unreal.

Admittedly, a vampire has many powers. It is usually very strong; bullets won't harm it; it can transform itself into a bat, and it can use the power of hypnosis to lull its victims. But, to balance this, the poor rascals can't resist sunlight, a cross, garlic, holy water, or a stake through the heart. So, in the case of vampires, the monster's powers are balanced by weaknesses.

Whatever powers you decide to give your monster, always leave room for its defeat by *human* means. Your hero must have an honest chance to overcome whatever menace is being faced in order to satisfy reader demand for a legitimate climax.

Once you have given your monster certain powers, you must stick to these throughout the story or novel. You won't be playing fair with the reader if, in the last part of your narrative, the monster suddenly reveals a brand new power you've just decided he needs. The reader must know the rules of your monster game—and once these rules are established, cheating is not permitted. Your werewolf can't suddenly sprout a pair of wings in chapter thirty and flap away over the treetops to escape the police.

Conversely, you can't establish a monster's weakness and then reverse it during your story. If your sheriff shoots the werewolf with a silver bullet and the bullet does no harm, you can't get away with, at this point, telling your reader that *your* werewolf is impervious to silver bullets. Silver bullets are supposed to kill werewolves. Therefore, you're not playing by the rules.

Horrific Humans

Finally, let's talk a bit more about *human* monsters. If you make your monster a "normal" human, how do you keep this person from being merely criminal . . . instead of monstrous?

You might start by reading *Red Dragon* and *The Silence of the Lambs* by Thomas Harris. In both of these books, the author creates very human monsters—most notably, a character called Dr. Hannibal Lecter, who is urbane, witty, extremely well educated, and seductively charming (when it suits his purpose). He is also capable of horrendous acts:

> *Lecter's shoulder drove the iron door into him, Pembry going for the Mace in his belt, his arm mashed to his body by the door. Lecter grabbed the long end of the baton and lifted. With the leverage twisting Pembry's belt tight around him, he hit Pembry in the throat with his elbow and sank his teeth in Pembry's face. Pembry trying to claw at Lecter, his nose and upper lip caught between the tearing teeth. Lecter shook his head like a rat-killing dog and pulled the riot baton from Pembry's belt. In the cell Boyle bellowing now, sitting on the floor, digging desperately in his pocket for his handcuff key, fumbling, dropping it, finding it again. Lecter drove the end of the baton into Pembry's stomach and throat and he went to his knees. Boyle got the key in a lock of the handcuffs, he was bellowing, Lecter coming to him now. Lecter shut Boyle up with a shot of the Mace and as he wheezed, cracked his upstretched arm with two blows of the baton. Boyle tried to get under the table, but blinded by the Mace he crawled the wrong way and it was easy, with five judicious blows, to beat him to death.*

With Dr. Lecter, the author shows us a man without human compassion or guilt, a man who is so savage that he transcends what we think of as criminal behavior. Lecter is not merely a normal man turned murderous: he has become a true monster in human form.

With his novel *Marathon Man*, William Goldman gives us another human monster, Christian Szell, an elegant fiend who had performed dreadful experiments in dentistry on Jewish prisoners at Auschwitz. Suddenly recognized in postwar New York, Szell reveals his killing savagery:

> *"I knew you weren't English, you murdering son of a bitch," and Szell, as he felt his body turning, flicked his Cutter down, and by the time he faced the fat man, it was already moving, one quick, almost imperceptible gesture with his right hand and the fat man's throat was suddenly and totally laid open, and as the fat man started to fall forward, grabbing for his jugular, Szell began shouting, "There's a sick man here, there's a man here needs help, a doctor, please a doctor," and as the fat man fell over the railing, almost already dead, a crowd gathered, and by the time the fat man could no longer hold his hands around*

his throat and dropped them, by the time the blood began to faucet, he was surrounded by many people, most of them screaming and none of them Szell, who was half running toward an empty cab.

If you wish to frighten your reader by creating such a monster in fleshly form, then you must invest the character with an emotional aura of total evil. The normal emotions and feelings shared by most of us must be missing in your character—or if these feelings *are* present, they must be twisted and perverted to a degree that removes the character from a common emotional reference point.

In my novel *Helltracks*, I present such a monster, Edward Timmons, who only *seems* normal in a surface sense. He talks (in his notebook) about moral values and healthful habits; he abhors swearing and sexually related slang; he is put off at the sight of blood, claiming he cannot abide violence in any form.

Yet this man is a compulsive strangler who dispatched his first victim at the age of twelve. He is always able to rationalize his murderous acts:

> *We all have to die, right? So when I strangle somebody (and I always pride myself on doing a good, quick job), it's not so terrible because that person is going to be dead anyway and it could well be that I have saved them from getting cancer or AIDS or having a whole series of painful heart attacks. Or from having a stroke. (Did you ever see pictures of somebody paralyzed all over so that only their eyes move?) . . .*
>
> *When I kill, and this is a real important point to be made, I do it in a very clean fashion. In a pure way, with my hands. I make direct personal contact. It's like an act of communion between me and the one I strangle.*

Credibility Is the Key

Thus, summing up, the monsters you create for your stories and novels must be credible; whether human or supernatural or robotic (the gunfighter in *Westworld*; the avenger from the future in *The Terminator*). They must pose a significant threat to your main characters. They must be removed from the norm. And they must *not* be all-powerful.

So pick your monster. Werewolf? Vampire? Zombie? Ghoul? Demon? Witch? Robot? Serial killer?

The choice is yours.

Just keep them scary — and *real*.

3.
HORRIBLE IMAGININGS

Horror is all around us. It fills the news of the day. Woman kidnapped and killed. School bus tumbles over cliff. Terrorist attack destroys church. Commercial airliner goes down in mountains. Cancer claims more victims. Coed brutally raped on campus. Police officer shot in drug sweep. Border raid wipes out village. . . .

We have all lived real-life horrors. Let me cite just one from my life. In Kansas City, where I was born and raised, I lived for nineteen years in a small house on Forest Avenue. During this entire period, our next door neighbors, Arthur and Adele Joergens, were like a second set of parents to me. Their marriage was childless, and I was the son they never had. Each summer I spent two weeks with them at a lake cabin they owned, and these annual trips were among the highlights of my childhood.

In 1947, when I was nineteen, my father was offered a job in California. We sold the house at 3337 Forest Avenue for a move to the West Coast. We said goodbye to Arthur and Adele. They were devastated; we were severing deep emotional roots. It was a painful leave-taking for everyone.

In California a year passed without word from them. We were concerned with this lack of contact, especially in view of the fact that Adele had told my mother (just before we left Missouri) that she didn't know what to do with Arthur, who had been undergoing severe emotional problems.

Finally we got the news in a clipping from the *Kansas City Star*. Arthur and Adele had engaged in a bitter quarrel. He had taken out a gun and fired at her. Wounded, she rushed to the kitchen door and tried to unlock it. He followed her into the kitchen and fired the gun again, killing her. No one heard the shots. He then went outside and watered the lawn.

Returning to the house, he took out a kitchen knife and cut his own throat. His body fell across hers against the locked door. The corpses were found when a relative came to visit them two days later and noticed bullet holes in the screen. The murder/suicide was headline news in Kansas City.

Horror. Surrounding us. Day by day, hour by hour. A strong reason, I am convinced, why horror fiction and horror films are so popular and effective. They provide mass therapy, a way to deal with the everyday horrors we all encounter.

Horror fiction offers us a way to *survive*. We are able to *control* the horror in a way we can never do in real life.

How do you separate genuine horror, the kind you'll be writing about, from that which is merely sad, or unpleasant, or disgusting?

It's all a matter of approach and degree. There are no set rules as to what is fit to write about and what isn't. Sad and disgusting things can and do often form the basis for tales of the horrific. What may strike one writer as a subject for horror might repel another. It boils down to a matter of personal taste, personal excitation.

Under the all-encompassing umbrella of horror fiction, almost any theme is possible to write about. The only real limit is your own imagination.

War is often sad and disgusting, yet the horrors of Vietnam have formed the basis for some excellent genre fiction. Example: Robert McCammon's classic *Nightcrawlers*, in which dead soldiers from Vietnam converge on a roadside diner.

Basically, horror fiction is meant to entertain and to deliver some delicious chills along the way. In this context, real-life horrors are certainly the most difficult to present as entertainment. If your protagonist is dying of AIDS, the situation is so hopeless and depressing that the reader becomes deeply uncomfortable. Therefore, it's best to create a horror of your own devising that is less emotionally painful. A dying vampire works much better than a dying cancer patient.

What then, might best serve you as a basis for your work?

Your Childhood as Inspiration

Human fear is the primary force behind a great deal of horror fiction.

The fears of our childhood offer rich source material. Remember how scary it was in your room late at night with all the lights off, how vulnerable and helpless you felt there alone under the covers? What Awful Thing was lurking in the closet ready to leap out at you? And what horror was hiding under your bed, ready to bite off your fingers if you let your arm dangle over the side of the mattress?

There are numerous stories in the genre dealing with such fears. Stephen King's "The Boogeyman" conjures up every child's nightmare (we were *all* afraid of the Boogeyman, right?). In masterly fashion, King makes this imaginary creature real for us. And in "The Chimney," Ramsey Campbell dramatizes the fear of what-might-be-hiding-in-the-chimney.

Children often fear adults, and this fear sometimes extends to their parents. What if their parents *changed*, became alien and evil?

I explored this fear in my story "The Halloween Man." At the end of the narrative, my protagonist, a little girl named Katie, thinks that the evil spirit of a Halloween monster has taken over her father's body. Because of this, she is terrified of him. Was her fear justified? Or was this *change* all in her mind? I leave it for the reader to decide.

Adult change, or possession, forms the basis for Jack Finney's *Invasion of the Body Snatchers*, wherein alien pods hatch out to replicate the form of their human victims.

Countless horror stories have been written on the theme of "what is real and what is illusion" or "what is human and what is alien." (This question formed the basis for the entire works of Philip K. Dick.)

Again, the possible variations for new horror fiction on the theme are literally inexhaustible.

What were you most afraid of as a child? A giant spider? A prowling ghost? A toy of yours coming to life? The family cat turning into a ravenous tiger? Your parents moving away and leaving you behind? Dig back in your mind and bring out the thing that frightened you most. Then write about it. Put that fear into a story. Make it as real as you can manage; attempt to reexperience that long-ago fear. Make your readers experience it right along with you. It will remind them of childhood fears of their own.

Grown-up Fears: Universal and Personal

Successful horror deals with our primal fears — of darkness, of being abandoned, of dangerous creatures, and, most often, of death itself.

The fear of death lies at the heart of almost all horror fiction, and the ways you can deal with it as a writer are endless. The threat of death will never go out of fashion; it is, in fact, humankind's *ultimate* fear. When your protagonist defeats the menace that threatens his or her life, you offer the reader the illusion that Mr. Death can be overcome—at least for the duration of your story or novel. This is one of the primary reasons people enjoy horror on the screen or on the printed page. They can face death and overcome it; they have *survived* with your hero, where others (in your story as well as in real life) have not.

What other fears motivate adults?

There are many—and each offers you rich source material for horror. The fear of being lost, of waking up alone and helpless in some remote spot; the fear of becoming old and feeble; the fear that people are not what they seem, that no one else in the world is real—or that you are surrounded by potential enemies.

Richard Matheson made a career out of exploring his personal paranoia, fictionally dramatizing it in story after story. Matheson feared getting caught in a "speed trap" while driving through a small town. In his story "The Children of Noah," the protagonist is arrested, taken from his car, and placed in the local jail. He ends up being literally devoured by the townspeople. In "Duel," which launched Steven Spielberg's career when he filmed the story for television, a giant truck with an unseen driver relentlessly pursues an innocent, terrified motorist—to the point of destruction—for no apparent reason. (Another Matheson view of life's random insanity.)

Ask yourself: What things frighten me as an adult?

These need not always be monstrous forms or evil creatures. Charles Beaumont was afraid of roller coasters. What delights most amusement-park roller-coaster riders terrified Beaumont. As a writer, he put his fear into action with "Perchance to Dream," in which the protagonist is taken on a terrifying roller-coaster ride by a female death figure.

We all have special, inner fears. Locate your own—then write about them. They'll be all the more real to your readers since they are so very real to you.

Do you have a fear of heights?

Do furry black insects make your skin crawl?

Do you sometimes feel trapped in the tight confines of an elevator?

The answers to such questions are the stuff of salable horror fiction.

Your Dream World Transformed

The most common question asked of professional writers is, Where do you get your ideas?

Well, the exploration of childhood and adult fears is one way to come up with a multitude of story ideas.

Our dreams provide another excellent source.

Mary Shelley claimed that her classic *Frankenstein* was based on a vivid dream, and a series of dreams inspired Robert Louis Stevenson to write *Dr. Jekyll and Mr. Hyde*.

Some of my best horror story ideas have come from dreams. Usually, you don't have the whole plot supplied to you in a dream—or if you do, the plot doesn't always hold up the next day. But sometimes you get lucky. The entirety of my story "He Kilt It With a Stick" came from a very vivid nightmare.

In this dream, I was walking home at night in Kansas City with only half a block left to reach my house. I became aware of cats. Hundreds of cats. All around me. In the street, on porches, in trees, on the tops of cars . . . everywhere. I began to run, knowing they would come after me, that they wanted to kill me. I reached the door of my house with the cat horde right behind me. Got the door unlocked, but—too late—the creatures were upon me in a clawing, biting mass. The last thing in my dream was the killing scream of the cats.

I woke up sweating. That same day, I wrote "He Kilt It With a Stick." All I needed to invent was a *reason* for my protagonist to be attacked. And I came up with the idea that he was a cat-hater, always had been, and that he had "kilt" cats with a stick even as a child. As an adult, he continued to destroy them—until one dark night they all banded together to exact their revenge. I then wrote the scene almost entirely as I had dreamed it. (And by the way, I'm no cat-hater. We have three much-loved felines; I'm crazy about each of them.)

Usually, from dreams, you get only ideas or scenes. "Lonely Train A 'Comin' " had its genesis in a dream. I awoke with the image of a cowboy sitting alone on a remote, windswept railway depot platform on the plains of Montana, waiting for a train. In my dream, the train was evil, and he was waiting to destroy it. I not only got a strong short story out of this, but ended up using it nine years later as the basis for my first horror novel, *Helltracks*. And I'm not the only one who has taken advantage of dream images and scenes: several writers I know have told me that dreams are an important supply source for their fiction.

When we sleep, our subconscious is free to take us anywhere it pleases. There are no rational limits, no restrictions on where we go or what happens to us. Sequences, locales, and images often become very bizarre — ideal as the setting for tales of terror. The dream state offers us rides Disneyland could never match. Anything goes.

Having a note pad handy is essential. Your conscious mind will *not* retain what you have dreamed. Your dreams will mist away within fifteen minutes after awakening unless you've jotted down the details to lock them into place. Occasionally you'll wake up, grab your note pad, and draw a blank; you know you had a great dream, but it's already gone. However, the more you train yourself to record what you *can* remember, the more you *will* remember.

Your Notebook as Collaborator

Another jump: from note pad to notebook.

I'm a nut for notebooks. I feel that it is absolutely vital for writers to use them. Yours can be a small one that fits easily into a pocket; or it can be a larger, 8½ × 11 version with hard covers (the kind I use); or it can be pages in a three-ring binder. Whichever works best for you.

What should go into your notebook? Well, I'll tell you what goes into mine (and so far I've filled eight of them):

plot ideas
scraps of overheard conversations
descriptions: people, places, things
bits of personal philosophy and insights
potential story and book titles
travel notes
research data
scenes (complete with dialogue)
statistics and odd facts
verse
childhood memories
things loved and hated

capsule movie reviews
critical opinions
notes taken from TV, newspapers, and magazines
character sketches

Think of your notebook as your writing collaborator. It records the immediate inner life of your mind, and the material you place in it will often emerge later in your written work. (It surely does in mine.) Those notes and plot ideas turn into stories; those bits of isolated dialogue may be perfect for one of your future characters; that odd fact or bit of research data will be just the thing you need to complete a scene.

Take your notebook with you—to work, to the library, and on social occasions when you go out to dinner or a show. Take it with you on trips and vacations—or to the beach on a hot Sunday afternoon. Carrying it should become as natural as carrying a wallet or a purse. You just never know when a thought, image, or idea will surface in your mind; if you fail to write it down, it's likely to be permanently lost.

A small cassette recorder (you can get them with built-in microphones) can also be very effective, serving as a kind of audio notebook, and there are writers who prefer to use this verbal method of preserving thoughts and ideas. It's up to you.

The Do-It-Yourself Ending

Since I'm still on the subject of generating plot ideas, I'll tell you another way to do it. Pick up a new anthology of horror tales and read only the first half of each story. Then put the story aside and write down your ideas on how the second half should go, with *your* version of the ending. Then go back and read the rest of the printed story. You'll be surprised to find that many times your sequence of events and your ending will be quite different from the printed version. Then all you have to do is discard what you read and create your own first half to go with your new second half.

Warning: This doesn't always work, since your story may end up being a ripoff of the original, simply a variation on what you read. However, on occasion, you emerge with a terrific new tale of your own that has only a distant relationship to the printed story that inspired it. In either case, the things you'll learn about structure and plotting make this experiment well worthwhile.

One Writer's Seedbed of Ideas

The prolific genre novelist J.N. Williamson compiled a list of supernatural belief systems that he uses as background for his fiction. I am certain you also will profit from this list, since it's a veritable seedbed for horror ideas:

1. Reincarnation; evil's embodiment (the Antichrist); friendship and individualism.
2. Voodoo; self-sacrifice; individualism over corporate autonomy.
3. Thought projection/generation; the sanctity of the family.
4. ESP, the paranormal; occult soul living in burial mound; love.
5. Apparatus with which to contact the dead; sacrifice for the common good.
6. Judgment Day; the Second Coming; spontaneous human combustion; God's intervention.
7. Mythology; feminism.
8. Ghosts and seances; *ephialtes* and *bruxa*; family life/survival.
9. Transmogrification and immortality; rights of the living taking precedence over those of the dead.
10. Fairies (leprechauns, banshees, the nuckalavee); ancestor worship; romantic love.
11. Vampires; psychic archeology; levity as a means to sanity.
12. Psychic combat; telepathy; well-applied human courage and know-how.
13. UFO; hypnotic regression; invasion by another world; individual human brain power over arrogant underestimations.
14. Ghouls, ghosts; levitation; parental self-sacrifice.
15. Astrology; the *lamia*; witchcraft; living statues.
16. Mind manipulation; alien invasion; familial unity as strength.
17. Biologically engineered vampire infants; primal source.
18. Egyptian magic; the talisman; parental bravery.
19. Zoroastrianism; Atlantis; innocence of small children.
20. Mummification; androgyny; sibling sacrifice; the question of intellectual superiority.
21. A ghost's human loneliness; errors of Heaven and Hell; ESP; tunnel to the other side.
22. Earthbound spirits, good and evil; ice-beasts; methodology of the dead returning to life.

Your Life Experience = Ideas

But, you ask, what if I run out of ideas? What then?

Relax. Take my word, it's a false worry. Your problem, once you get rolling, will be finding the time to put all of your ideas into finished form. I've known dozens of professional writers, and I have never—repeat *never*—encountered one who didn't have an overflowing idea file.

Ideas, happily enough, are everywhere. They're floating all around you. You don't have to look in exotic places to find them, since life itself offers an endless supply. Ideas are most often obtained from the commonplace, the ordinary. Your house. Your family. Your friends. Your job. Your hobbies. And, of course—that rich seedbed—your childhood. And since we are all totally different individuals, no one else on this planet has experienced life exactly as you have. Instead of expending so much energy trying to imitate other writers (as most beginners do), put your energy into exploring yourself and the world around you.

Idea into Plot

So you have your idea. How do you work it into a salable story? What are the stages in development from basic idea to completed manuscript?

First you must turn your idea into a plot.

Suppose you have come up with the simple idea of a man trapped in an elevator. That's your *seed* idea, nothing else.

You begin by asking yourself questions.

How *long* is this fellow going to be trapped in the elevator? At least twenty-four hours, you decide. Can't be much longer or he would die there. No water (or food) on an elevator.

Why does it take so long to rescue him? Old office building. It's going to be torn down soon. He's the last tenant. On his final trip up to fetch his boxed belongings. No one else in the building.

What *happens* while he's in the elevator? He undergoes a total life change. For the first time in years, he is forced to "stand still," to *think* about his life. During these long hours inside the cage of the elevator, he is forced to confront the fact that his frantic, workaholic lifestyle is destroying his family. He's not been spending nearly enough time with the kids; one of them is into drugs, the other is having trouble at school. And his wife is drinking heavily when he's away on his frequent trips, working on yet another of his out-of-town deals. They seldom make love anymore; the bond between them has almost vanished because of his absence.

Now you have something. By the time a passing cop rescues him, your protagonist has undergone a complete alteration; he vows to change the focus of his business so he can stay in town and have proper time with his family.

So—these are your three stages—your beginning (he goes into the building and gets trapped in the elevator), your middle (his thoughts—and the various flashbacks to his frantically paced life), and your ending (he is freed from the elevator cage by the cop).

But is this a horror story? You bet. The horrors of being trapped for endless hours in total darkness, the fear that he may *die* there, that no one will come in time to save him. There's no vampire or werewolf in this one, but the story is genuine horror nonetheless. It could be very frightening to any reader who has ever feared getting trapped between floors. And hasn't that thought crossed the mind of all of us who use elevators?

What must be done, therefore, in making the successful transition from idea to finished manuscript is to ask yourself a variety of pertinent questions about your character (or characters), your locale, the particular threat facing your protagonist, and the way the threat is finally resolved.

Trust your subconscious. It will provide answers for you all along the way. The middle of your story will form itself naturally from your beginning and your ending.

You'll be surprised to find all these answers inside your mind. I am constantly surprised at what comes up when I dip into this well of self. And it's true with every writer I've known.

Ideas.

Questions.

Answers.

It's really just that basic.

4.
WHO – OR WHAT – GOES THERE?

In a horror novel or short story, there is one primary rule that I'll set right up front: Make your characters as realistic as possible.

Reality is your bridge into the fantastic. If readers empathize with your characters and truly believe in them as projections of real life, then they will follow them into whatever fantastic situations you provide. You will achieve what Coleridge termed "the willing suspension of disbelief." Your reader will *want* to believe your story, no matter how improbable it may be in objective reality.

Consider King's novel *The Shining*. The author takes a full one hundred pages before his characters reach the Overlook Hotel, where the major horrors begin. King wanted to establish the Torrance family in three-dimensional depth, making them as real as the reader's own family. He detailed their business and social life, dramatized their personal problems, and delved into their past. He allowed them to live and breathe on the page in order to gain the reader's total confidence. Then, and only then, did he send them into the haunted hotel to meet their bloody fate, knowing that the reader, now emotionally hooked, would follow them anywhere.

Examine any really successful horror novel and you will encounter fully fleshed characterization. If it is *not* there, the book will sell poorly and quickly disappear. Genre novelist Robert R. McCammon sums it up: "Humanity is what's missing from bad horror fiction."

To inject this level of reality/humanity into your work, you must *believe* in the people you're writing about. This kind of confidence can't be faked; the emotions you present in your characters must be genuine, rooted in the daily conflicts and problems we all face.

T.E.D. Klein (former editor of *Twilight Zone Magazine*) said: "Whatever his personal convictions, while writing his horror tale, the author must believe in it . . . performing the same magic on himself that he hopes to perform upon the reader."

Know Your Characters

Before you begin to write a horror novel, you must prepare fully fleshed-out biographies for your main characters. These will include your protagonist, your villain (who is, in most horror tales, the monster), and any subsidiary characters (good *or* evil) who are important to the narrative. Minor characters who appear simply in walk-on capacities (the cop who directs traffic on the corner, the neighborhood mail carrier, the proprietor of the local Mom-and-Pop grocery store where your protagonist buys the daily paper) do not need full biographies.

I suggest that you put down each character's name on a 4" × 6" file card and then ask yourself a series of questions about the character. Your written answers (use as many cards as you need for them) will form the authentic background from which your story will be drawn.

If you have several important characters who need complete biographies, you may want to color-code your cards, using one color for your protagonist, another for your villain, another for important subsidiary characters, and yet another for people in walk-on roles. This becomes a convenient system if you have more than a dozen characters in your novel. (Short stories, because they *are* short, usually have only two or three characters.)

The information you put on these cards will vary with your concept and your characters; there is no standard format writers use.

In my novel *Helltracks*, it was important to emphasize the differences between my protagonist, Josh Ventry, and his girlfriend, Cris Mitchell. Therefore, I had to determine where each grew up (he in a tiny town in rural Montana; she in sophisticated Tucson, Arizona), their educational backgrounds (he never went beyond high school; she is a college graduate and licensed engineer), as well as lifestyle differences (he's barely traveled beyond the confines of Montana; she's been around the world twice). When the novel opens, they are natural antagonists, on opposite sides of a public environmental controversy that affects them both. By the time the novel ends, they are united, both personally and environmentally. This major character change had to be logical, so I had to determine what biographical elements would convey character transformation most efficiently in the case of these two particular people. Because Josh was the son of rural sheep ranchers and Cris was the daughter of a multimillionaire, I had to determine what each would eat (since food is such a powerful indicator of social class and lifestyle), think, and feel. Their hobbies and habits (Josh's interest in American Indian mystical traditions, Cris's collection of fortunes from Chinese fortune cookies) were important.

In contrast, in my novel *Logan's Run*, I didn't go into detail about food, travel, education, hobbies, habits, or hometown in regard to my characters' backgrounds or lifestyles. None of these things was necessary in *Logan's Run*, and none would have conveyed vital character information. The main characters in that story were broadly drawn, typical of their culture and situation, rather than highly individualized. Therefore, it would have been a waste of time for me to include any of these items in their biographies.

What's in a Name?

The names you give your characters are important. Every name conveys an emotional image. Psychological studies have repeatedly proved that people have definite perceptions of particular names. Although these may change with the times (Ethel, Hazel, and Blanche were considered sexy names for attractive young women in the 1920s), in any particular era there is general agreement about what specific names mean. Therefore, you want to choose each character's name to enhance the reality of that person in your reader's mind. You don't want to mislead your readers by using names that work against the image you seek to convey, or that fail to reflect the nature of particular characters in your story.

Don't call a tough private eye Erwin or Percy. Sure, Bogart's first name in real life was Humphrey, but nobody ever called him that. They called him Bogie. Why? Because Bogie was a perfect fit for his tough-guy image.

And don't worry about what particular people may be called in real life. That sensuous blonde in the skintight satin pants at the bar might be named Matilda, or even Hortense, but in your story, either of those names would be misleading. You'd do better calling her Ava or Yvonne or Chantal.

The menace in your story should *sound* mean. In one of my novels, I named my villain Gant. The name is hard and edged, just like the character. Stephen King named his villain in *The Dark Half* Stark—a harsh, hard name for a harsh, hard man. And the evil boy in Robert R. McCammon's *Mystery Walk* is named Falconer, suggesting a frightening bird of prey.

Avoid names that rhyme in the same story, Dick/Rick . . . Ellen/Helen . . . Harry/Larry. Rhyming names create confusion in the mind of your readers; they find it difficult to distinguish Larry from Harry.

Avoid such highly recognizable public names as Elvis or Hemingway. In most cases, readers will be reminded of the celebrity, not the character in your story.

Be aware of differences due to chronological age, geography, social class, religion, and ethnic group, because American names are not distributed evenly or randomly. Instead, most names cluster. You'll find lots of Dwaynes in the working-class South, hardly any among the students or professors at Harvard or Yale. Italian-Americans named Tony are heavily represented in the Northeast; men answering interchangeably to Juan or John are common in the Southwest. Jennifer and Jason are popular names for those born in the 1970s and 1980s, but you'd be hard put to find either name listed in the high school graduation classes of the 1940s and 1950s. Debutantes are commonly named Melissa, Catherine, and Alison; beauty school students are commonly named Penny and Cindy and Pattie Lee.

Where do you find the right names for your characters? The phone book is a convenient source, and out-of-town phone books are an available source for names common in specific geographic areas. (Your public library should have a reference collection of out-of-town phone books.) Newspapers are also good sources, especially for geographically correct names. Upper-class names are found in the society pages; middle-class names are found in the listings of community activities; working- and lower-class names (and names for elderly people) are found in the obituaries and legal columns.

Important: Never, ever use the full names of real people! This could lead to unpleasant legal consequences. Instead, take a first name that fits from one real person, then a last name that fits from another real person. Put them together and you've got the name of your character.

Constructing the Protagonist

Each story or novel must feature a *protagonist*. This is your main character. He or she dominates the action and is the person around whom the major conflict is centered. It is the protagonist who meets the story's monster head-on in your climax and (usually) defeats it.

In many cases, the protagonist is an adult male, but females often serve as the central character (Ripley from the *Alien* series, as portrayed by Sigourney Weaver, is a prime example). Sometimes it's a child (Danny in King's *The Shining*), while occasionally other creatures serve in this capacity—the robot in Alfred Bester's horror/science fiction tale "Fondly Fahrenheit," or an alien beast (Coeurl in A.E. Van Vogt's "Black Destroyer"). In Bradbury's "There Shall Come Soft Rains," the protagonist is a fully automated house.

However, because the vast majority of horror stories feature human protagonists, I shall assume that you will be pitting your monsters against flesh-and-blood heroes. (Protagonists are not *always* heroes—but heroes are always protagonists.)

How do you construct an effective and appropriate human protagonist?

To be convincing, this person must be someone with whom the reader can identify, be sympathetic toward, be concerned about, empathize with, and root for in time of crisis. In a word, the character must be plausible.

Plausibility in a fictional character can be achieved in several ways.

Let's say you decide to make your protagonist a businessman; he becomes involved with a devil cult, ultimately must battle with its leader, and ends up destroying the cult at the novel's climax.

First, you must decide what *type* of business your protagonist is in, and then provide enough details about that business to give it an aura of authenticity. In *Helltracks*, my protagonist, Josh Ventry, works for his father on the family's Montana sheep ranch. I did a great deal of research on sheep ranching in order to supply Josh with a believable background. When I began, I knew absolutely *nothing* about sheep—beyond the fact that they bleated and were woolly—but by the time I wrote the novel, I had learned a great deal, and I was able to put this knowledge into my narrative, lending authenticity to Josh Ventry's life.

When you're researching a character's work background, you usually end up with far more information than your story requires. You must then select what parts of the material to include in order to create a fully authentic portrait.

Your hero must have at least one weakness (his Achilles' heel) that can be exploited by the enemy. You are not creating clones of Superman or Wonder Woman. A weakness lends humanity to your character. It will also provide suspense; this particular weakness may often lead to a near-defeat at your book's end. And remember, I said *near*-defeat. In the final conflict, your hero should emerge triumphant to "pay off" your drama. At least, this is true in most horror novels; many short stories end darkly. In short fiction, readers haven't invested so much time and sympathy in the characters and story that anything less than victory at the end is emotionally unacceptable — a letdown, a disappointment. Short stories can support grim endings; generally, novels can't.

Your protagonist could be physically handicapped. (In Michael Collins's crime novels, private detective Dan Fortune has lost an arm.) Or the character could have a mental hang-up that might surface at a critical moment. In my teleplay "Bridge Across Time," my protagonist is an ex-Chicago cop who can no longer bring himself to fire a weapon because he shot and accidentally killed a fourteen-year-old back in Chicago. This act haunts his life. He can no longer bear guns of any kind. When he *must* shoot the villain at the climax in order to save the woman he loves, his finger freezes and he is in agonized conflict over pulling the trigger.

Your protagonist's weakness need be no more than ignorance — inexperience in the face of a critical situation that *demands* experience. Or simple callowness — youthful naiveté that the bad guys use to their advantage.

The point is to make your hero vulnerable. No human being is without flaws. Thus, to reflect the reality of life, your hero must be less than perfect.

How can you make readers identify with your protagonist? What traits should the character possess that will make your audience empathize?

Empathy is achieved when your character's thought processes and motivations are made clear and totally understandable. In *The Shining*, young Danny simply wants to find parental love; he wants his father to care for him the way his mother cares for him. But Jack Torrance is crazy (at least he goes very bonkers by the climax), and the only thing Danny can do at the end is run from him.

It's easy for the reader to identify with this sad, gifted little boy. In fact, Stephen King is not only a superb storyteller, he is a cunning master at character development. Any beginning writer would do well to study his novels and observe how King builds and maintains depth and believability in his people.

Give your protagonist some character flaws. For example, we all lose our temper from time to time, especially under extreme circumstances.

When your character is stressed, allow him or her to exhibit similar break points.

Another example: In life, we often deceive ourselves; we, in effect, tell lies to ourselves in order to pursue unwise goals (such as buying some high-calorie confection "for the family" when you're the only one who really likes this particular treat). Therefore, your character might be guilty of some degree of self-deception. This could lead to plot complications, as well as roadblocks along the way as your protagonist attempts to defeat the monster.

You must build normal, human traits into your protagonist so that readers will recognize aspects of themselves in your fictional creation.

Always remember that your protagonist must be *consistent*. You cannot arbitrarily bend the character out of shape and have him or her do things that are inconsistent with this character's personality because you wish to reach a certain plot point.

For example, let's say you create a character who had a near-fatal childhood accident falling from a barn. Therefore, he has developed a vivid fear of heights. You cannot then have this character, in a pursuit scene during the climax, casually chase the villain over rooftops. If the chase *must* take place from a height, then your protagonist should be apprehensive and suffer great fear during the pursuit (James Stewart in Hitchcock's *Vertigo*). The protagonist's behavior throughout the story must conform to the *type* of character you have created.

He or she must also emotionally relate to the other people in your story. As Dean Koontz said, "Fiction is about the interaction of people, about their complex relationships."

Create a Compassionate Character

Your protagonist must *care* about others. Your character must act not only to preserve his or her own life (the instinct of self-survival being central to our nature), but to preserve the lives of those he or she has come to love. A spouse. A child. An animal.

And, if your protagonist is a mature and healthy human being, then this character will act to preserve the lives of any person (or any creature) he or she feels responsible for. Many situations arise in life when people take responsibility for total strangers, whether those strangers be human or animal. Doing so is routine in emergencies. An auto accident. A fire.

34

An earthquake. All elicit instant response from total strangers, who stop whatever they're doing to help those in need. A dog gets stranded on a piece of ice floating down a winter river. A cat gets caught in a water pipe. A whale swims the wrong way into San Francisco Bay. A bear wanders from the mountains into a big city, or sea animals get caught in the goo of an oil spill, and suddenly entire communities are galvanized into compassionate action. Why? Because the individuals in those communities feel *responsible*; they are in a position to help, and therefore they feel the inner *obligation* to help. This is one of the prime characteristics of healthy, mature, fully functioning human beings.

This caring for others can be developed gradually within your narrative. In my novel *Logan's Run*, the protagonist initially makes his run for a selfish purpose—to destroy the "Sanctuary Line" (which allows rebels to escape from a computer-dictated early death), and thus reestablish order in the system. But during his run, Logan learns how to love, as his relationship to Jessica, sister of a man he's killed, deepens and expands. This love alters him; he begins to realize the possibility of a future life, beyond and outside the system, for him and Jessica—that they can raise a family and grow old together, eventually dying natural deaths. Thus, his run becomes a run *toward* Sanctuary, rather than an attempt to destroy it.

Character Change Is Crucial

The events of your story *must* cause your protagonist to change. In most cases, this means that your character matures beyond the point of his or her entrance into the story. If your narrative is to have depth and realism, your protagonist cannot emerge from the events of the story personally unaltered. Lessons must have been learned. Emotions must have been deepened. The character's basic approach to life must have been altered because of the trials and dangers encountered en route.

Sometimes this change can be physical as well as emotional. It is possible to put your character through events so grueling that he or she is brought to the point of near extinction. As the novel comes to its end, your character may be taken to a point just this side of death itself. In the Bond novels, Ian Fleming did this to his secret agent time and again. By the final chapter, having defeated the villain, Bond was often a physical wreck. Yet he survived—a bit more wary, a bit more mature.

In making things tough for your hero, you not only add to the suspense, you demonstrate your protagonist's strength and qualities of endurance. Your protagonist must struggle to achieve a happy ending; the task must never be easy. The more difficult his or her struggle, the more satisfying the triumph.

Of course, not all endings are happy ones — but I'll be dealing with endings at greater length in Chapter Eleven.

Creating a believable protagonist depends on the various levels of depth you build into the character.

Cardboard heroes no longer make the grade in today's popular fiction market. Your reader wants to follow a protagonist who demonstrates strength, intelligence, and compassion — and who matures into a better person because of the events of your story.

It is your job to provide such a character.

Passivity Is Out

Let's talk about the *role* of your main character. What does he or she have to do in order to dominate the story and fulfill the basic requirements of a true protagonist?

First of all, your central character should be active, not passive. The character must act, not just react. He or she must personally resolve the conflict and face the menace. And no acts of God, please. No lightning from the sky that spears down to kill the horde of giant rats at the last moment. No sudden earthquake to swallow up the monster.

Your protagonist must be *directly* responsible for the defeat of whatever menace you provide in the story. He or she must be decisive, moving the action forward by well-motivated actions of mind and body. A weak, indecisive hero may be accepted in avant-garde literature, but such a character just won't cut the mustard in a popular horror tale. You don't need Rambo, but you can't get by with Walter Mitty, either. (Thurber's timid character was heroic *only* in his daydreams.)

Thus far, we've been dealing with main characters who are basically heroes — but what if your *monster* is the protagonist — as in *Frankenstein* and *Dr. Jekyll and Mr. Hyde*?

Readers will accept a monster as the main character of your story providing you are able to make these creatures at least *partially* sympathetic.

Certainly, with Jekyll and Hyde, there's no problem, since monster and hero occupy the same body. It's easy to feel sorry for poor Doc Jekyll as we see wily old Hyde take him over. At the story's climax, with the death of Hyde, the good doctor is back with us. A corpse, yes, but a *good* corpse.

With the big, shambling Monster in *Frankenstein*, there is much to pity; he is victim as well as killer. He is portrayed so masterfully by Boris Karloff in the original film version that the audience finds itself rooting for the poor clumsy fellow with the bolts in his neck who never asked to be created, and who is quite obviously more harried than harrying.

But what about Bram Stoker's *Dracula*? There are no qualities in that dark vampire with which to sympathize, right? Okay, right. Drac is one bad dude from start to finish. Yet *is* Dracula really the protagonist? The character of Van Helsing assumes that role, thus allowing Stoker to keep his blood-hungry count totally evil.

If you decide to make your monster the protagonist, then you would be wise to invest the creature with traits the reader can find sympathetic.

Harry Angel, the doomed private eye in William Hjortsberg's tour de force *Falling Angel* (a marvelous mix of the hard-boiled and the horrific) is a monster who gains our sympathy because of the fact that his own darker self is not revealed to him (or to us) until very late in the book. By then, we are 100 percent on Harry's side.

The vampire Lestat in the trilogy by Anne Rice is rendered sympathetic to us because of the author's ability to allow her readers to really *know* Lestat—as we live out his long bloody history down the centuries.

Hero versus Villain

Providing a strong, fully dimensional villain who can give your hero a real run for the money will make the hero's triumph all the more satisfying to readers.

Max Brand (pen name of the late Frederick Faust) nearly always created truly impressive villains for his Westerns. In his series of Silvertip novels, the outlaw Barry Christian was equally as potent and powerful as Brand's hero, and in Brand's Montana Kid series, the Mexican bandit, Meteo Rubriz, was a full match for the quick-shooting protagonist. And when they meet in climactic battle, the reader witnesses a clash of titans.

The greater the villain, the greater the hero.

Characters: Realistic But Not Real

Which leads to a question I have been often asked: Are your characters ever based on real people?

Yes. And no. I sometimes have the visual image of a real person in mind as I write, but usually this real person is simply a starting point. From that base of reality, I then change physical appearance, personality characteristics, mannerisms, and life history, so the character who eventually winds up in my story usually bears little resemblance to his or her real-life counterpart. I may also combine one real-life person with another—perhaps even with a third—adding in bits and pieces from all three.

In general, it's best to avoid an exact life-into-fiction rendition. You could be subject to libel suits, for one thing. And you certainly would be vulnerable to the anger and hurt of your friends and relatives. (Not to mention your boss, should you decide to portray him or her in your horror story!) It's more fun, and far more satisfying, to create your own fictional characters. *Use* real life, but don't attempt to duplicate it.

Once you have created a realistic character (protagonist or monster), you may be surprised to find that he or she will take off on a tangent as you write, doing things you hadn't planned or expected this character to do. That's fine. Allow yourself to follow the character, and you'll be led into some fresh, surprising scenes.

Actually, this is your subconscious at work, adding depth to what you have *consciously* planned. Naturally, there are limits; you have to keep your protagonist from straying too far from your ongoing plot. When Anne Rice got the idea for *Interview With the Vampire*, she thought it would turn out to be a short story. It became a long novel as the character literally took over. In fact, she realized that there was so much more to say about him and his world that she then wrote *The Vampire Lestat*, and with still more material crowding her mind, turned out a third novel, *The Queen of the Damned*—a perfect example of character takeover.

5.
DON'T OPEN THAT DOOR!

Suspense — a key word in the horror genre.

Any successful horror story contains a full measure — and with a fright novel, the suspense must be present throughout, reaching its apex at the narrative's climax.

How is suspense created and maintained?

Anticipation is the key to suspense. You are leading your reader toward what he or she *knows* is going to result in a dangerous confrontation with evil. You do it in careful stages, encouraging the reader to anticipate the horror, but holding it back, layering in other sequences that move your story forward but delay the actual climax the reader *knows* is coming.

If you have done the proper job of characterization, of making your readers *care* about the protagonist, then they will emotionally identify with the upcoming danger. But if readers don't believe in your characters, then they won't care what happens to them. For example, if you see a well-dressed stranger enter what you know to be a dangerous part of the city at night, you might think he's unwise or foolish, but you won't *worry* about him. His future situation is not your concern. You have no vested emotional interest in the man. As a writer, however, it is your task to create emotional bonding between reader and fictional character; this will result in audience identification and caring.

The descriptive words and phrases you use to build suspense are extremely important. They set the proper mood for the upcoming encounter.

In my story "Ceremony," I was very careful in my selection of suspense-laden words and phrases as I described my protagonist's first view of a special Rhode Island town:

> *He passed the dim-lit garage. In the gloom, standing next to a high-piled stack of discarded truck tires, a lean, unshaven mechanic in greased blood-dark overalls stared out at him.*
>
> *He continued along the street. The gravel gave way to concrete, but the ground was still uneven. Tufted grass spiked up from wide cracks in the surface. The ancient Victorian houses along the street were in equal disrepair, their gabled bay windows cracked and shadowed. Porches sagged. Roofs seemed hunched against the night.*
>
> *Doour's Mill had gone to seed, a time-worn New England relic of a town that seemed totally deserted.*

I'm setting the mood here. Impending horror. Note the use of such words and phrases as "dim-lit . . . gloom . . . blood-dark . . . cracked and shadowed . . . hunched against the night."

Not the kind of place you'd want to visit after dark. The reader knows by what I've written here that some Terrible Things are due to happen in Doour's Mill. Thus, suspense is generated.

Michael McDowell creates ongoing suspense in his multivolume novel, *Blackwater*, by presenting a seemingly ordinary housewife within the context of a normal Southern family whose dark powers allow her to change, quite suddenly, into a ghoulish eater of human flesh. The reader never knows when or under what circumstances this horrific transformation will occur—a guarantee of reader anticipation.

I used a similar technique with my serial killer in *Helltracks*. Most of the time he appears to have his compulsion under control, but the reader never knows when he may suddenly erupt into a killer. The anticipation, on the reader's part, is always there.

One primary method of creating suspense is to set up your threat early in the book. Something awful is going to happen if Bob and Jane honeymoon on a certain remote island. Why? Because you've let your readers know that this particular island is a very dangerous place. In your opening, another couple dies there in some horrible fashion. You don't reveal exactly what it was that killed them, but you do establish the threat posed by the mystery menace that occupies the island. Thus, you have created suspense. *What is going to happen when your newly married couple, Bob and Jane, oblivious to the horror that awaits them, decide to honeymoon on the island?*

At this point, you begin to build and deepen the suspense by bringing the menace closer. Let it attack Bob; he barely escapes. He attempts to get his wife off the island. More suspense as their boat is destroyed, trapping them. Next, the groom is *separated* from his new bride. She's lost on the island, and your menace is closing in on *her*. The suspense escalates as she falls and discovers she can't stand up again. Broken ankle. At the climax, just as it seems all is lost, Bob locates her, and in a battle to the death, he defeats the menace.

Suspense all the way.

I've used an overly simple plotline here to demonstrate how basic suspense may be layered into a narrative.

Your readers will stick with you so long as the outcome is uncertain. They will be trying to guess what's going to happen, so your job is to give the narrative a sudden twist that misleads. This creates surprise and continues the process of building suspense.

In a horror story, suspense ends when the monster is defeated, resulting in the removal of the threat. Until that moment, your readers must be kept off-balance; they must keep asking themselves: *What terrible thing is going to happen next? . . . And to whom?*

The threat cannot be false. It must pay off, and this means you must show your monster *in action*. Chewing up minor characters, for instance. This demonstrates to your audience exactly what this creature is capable of. You dramatize your creature's killing power in order to heighten the suspense of what will happen at the climax when hero and horror clash head-on. (Note how many victims the shark claims in *Jaws* before the beast is blown up at the climax.)

A warning: You must avoid overloading your narrative with too many consecutive scenes of shock and terror, one directly after another in an unbroken sequence. The shocks must be spaced far enough apart to give the reader some breathing space, and to allow the proper buildup of suspense that leads from one horrific sequence to the next. A jammed-together succession of shock sequences will result in plot overload; the shocks will cancel each other out in the reader's mind, and suspense will be defused and, ultimately, lost.

This principle is akin to one used in public speaking. I have delivered many lectures during my career, and I have learned to pause after a humorous or startling anecdote to give my audience a chance to react. Proceeding without these breaks creates an unpleasant tension. Spaced intervals must be provided so your audience can discharge emotions and release pent-up tension. Then, when the reader is relaxed again, you begin building to your next narrative climax.

I call this the roller-coaster method: a slow climb, a rapid, heart-stopping plunge, then another slow climb.

Setting your beleaguered protagonist to battle a series of dangerous obstacles is another method that can be used to create suspense. As your character encounters these barriers (both emotional and physical), the central conflict of the narrative is heightened.

Although the James Bond stories are not horror fiction per se, by the time Bond has finished his crawl through that long metal tunnel in *Dr. No*, he has been subjected to a horrible variety of tortures. The reader is with him every inch of the way, held in a thrall of taut suspense. *What will happen to 007 next?*

Approaching That Door: The Principle

One of the oldest forms of suspense in storytelling is the "Don't open that door!" principle. Your audience *knows* that something ghastly is waiting just inside the door—and here comes the hapless heroine down the long, dark hallway toward That Door. She stands outside and puts her hand on the knob . . . as your audience anxiously warns her: *"Don't open it!"* The suspense at that moment is intense because we know that if she *does* turn the knob, the Ghastly Thing inside will get her.

When I wrote my screenplay for the horror film *Burnt Offerings*, I utilized this age-old principle in getting Karen Black and her family out of the Awful House. Will they get out alive? They seem to. At least, by the end, they are actually in the clear, outside, ready to drive away to safety—when suddenly Karen feels she must open the front door and *go back inside*. Oh, no! Suspense builds from the moment she leaves the car. We know that Something is waiting inside, in that evil place, ready to claim her forever. She must *not* open that door!

Again, let me cite a classic scene from King's *The Shining*, one of the key novels of horror in our century. There is a locked room in the Overlook Hotel, #217, that keeps drawing young Danny to it. Finally, he obtains the key and opens the door. At first, everything is normal, but then the boy sees a drawn shower curtain around the tub in the adjoining bathroom. He cautiously enters the bathroom, walks slowly to the tub—then draws back the curtain. In the bathtub is the dead, bloated corpse of a woman. As Danny watches, she *begins to move*. She sits up, her rotting, dead eyes staring at the boy.

Danny runs in terror, back to the now closed door. And here King delivers a sudden *reversal* of the "Don't open that door!" principle. He has his protagonist, on the *inside*, trying to *get out*.

> *He began hammering on [the door], far beyond realizing that it was unlocked, and he had only to turn the knob to let himself out. His mouth pealed forth deafening screams that were beyond human auditory range. He could only hammer on the door and hear the dead woman coming for him, bloated belly, dry hair, outstretched hands—something that had lain slain in that tub for perhaps years, embalmed there in magic.*
>
> *The door would not open, would not, would not, would not . . .*
>
> *His eyelids snapped down. His hands curled into balls. His shoulders hunched with the effort of concentration:*
>
> *(Nothing there nothing there not there at all NOTHING THERE THERE IS NOTHING!)*
>
> *Time passed. And he was just beginning to relax, just beginning to realize that the door must be unlocked and he could go, when the years-damp, bloated, fish-smelling hands closed softly around his throat and he was turned implacably around to stare into that dead and purple face.*

The suspense in this scene is thick enough to slice with a knife.

"It Was a Dark and Stormy Night . . . ": Isolation

Isolating your characters is another sure-fire method of creating suspense. Certainly, horror *can* strike at a character at high noon on Fifth Avenue in the middle of New York's congested lunch-hour traffic. (Actually, depending on how it's staged, such an unexpected attack can be highly effective.) But this is an exception. Horror is much more frightening when your characters are isolated and vulnerable. Then the reader feels they are at the mercy of the oncoming menace with nowhere to run, and with no one to help them. Suspense is greatly intensified.

Alfred Hitchcock's *Psycho* offers an ideal example of this. Here's Janet Leigh alone on the road. It is late night. A storm is upon her. Heavy, blinding rain. She looks for a place to stay to escape the storm. Finds this *isolated* motel, which just happens to be run by a madman. She takes a room. Undresses. Steps into the shower, where she is *totally vulnerable.* The madman enters, knife in hand, and attacks — stabbing her to death in the shower.

Here is suspense at its highest level. Once seen, this sequence is never forgotten.

In the film *Alien*, the heroine is isolated in a dark spaceship zillions of miles from Earth. All the other crew members have been done in by the Creature, and now she's all alone. What does she do? She takes off her clothes. She doesn't know the Creature is hiding in the same room. Thus, she is now *more* vulnerable. Without our clothing, we all feel far more defenseless, especially if we are facing any type of threat. Nakedness = vulnerability = suspense.

Consider the opening sequence in *Jaws*. Early morning. A swimmer alone (isolated) in the ocean, with no awareness of the oncoming danger. We see her white legs thrashing the water (vulnerable). Suddenly, horribly, she is struck by the shark and jerked underwater to her death. A grisly scene indeed, and one that brilliantly utilizes the elements I have been discussing.

In *The Shining*, Danny and his mother are isolated in a huge summer hotel that has been closed down for the winter. The roads are blocked with snow, and the two characters are vulnerable to the boy's father — who becomes homicidal, relentlessly stalking them both. Again, bad weather is used to heighten the suspense. That's why so many storms howl through horror literature; they help isolate the characters.

In *'Salem's Lot*, King isolates his characters in a small town in Maine, cut off from the kind of help a big city can provide. Around them, a slowly increasing horde of vampires! Small towns are always excellent locales for terror because characters in small towns are particularly vulnerable.

As I had one of my children declare in "The Halloween Man":

"He chased me once . . . in Havershim, Texas. Little bitty town, like this one. He likes small towns."
"How come?"

"Nowhere for kids to hide in a small town. Everything out in the open . . ."

Things That Go Bump in the Night

Darkness is also a great tool to utilize when you're building suspense. Darkness offers the ideal stage setting for Awful Things. Our characters can't see what's out there in the pitch black, waiting to gobble them up; the darkness isolates and cripples them.

Even with an element as familiar as darkness, there are always ways to be creative in its use. Find new, fresh locations in which darkness can add to the suspense. Not simply the expected darkness of a haunted house, but of an underground parking garage, or the interior of a rusting ship, or an office building full of slanting room shadows. Make that darkness so real in the reader's mind that he or she can feel it in the same way one feels an alien presence.

The Monster: Is It for Real?

One of the problems inherent in the creation of suspenseful horror fiction is the placement of *belief* within the narrative. What will convince the protagonist that the threat of the monster is real? What will convince other characters in the story? Should *everybody* believe in the monster?

Since most horror fiction deals with one form or another of the fantastic, it is vital that you prove to the reader that your Dark Menace is real. You do this in part by showing how your characters react to it. In the beginning, *nobody* believes in the monster. Even when a series of events occur that point directly to the monster, your protagonist should remain difficult to convince. But, as certain horrible events happen *just* to the protagonist, your character's skepticism gives way to partial belief. As events (and suspense) build, this develops into full belief.

In *Night of the Demon*, Dana Andrews begins the film as a total skeptic regarding supernatural powers—but by the film's climax, after a series of frightening events, he *knows* that it's all very real; the demon is indeed coming to rip him apart.

There is usually a point in almost every horror tale when *no one else* but your protagonist believes in the monster.

In the television series "Night Stalker," only the eccentric reporter, Carl Kolchak, actually believed in the bizarre monsters he pursued. His boss at the newspaper thought he was wacko; the police refused to believe him. He was lucky if, during the course of an episode, he could convince one or two others that the fantastic monster was real.

Never did *everyone* believe in the monster. And this is a hard-and-fast rule: Never allow *all* of the characters in your story to believe in the monster. Aside from the protagonist (and perhaps a few of his or her close associates), only the *victims* of the monster should totally accept the creature's reality. People are by nature skeptical — in real life as well as in fiction — and the majority of the characters in your story should remain skeptical in order to make the narrative credible.

The Terminator: The Epitome of Terror

Let me end this chapter with an examination of *The Terminator*, one of the most suspenseful terror-suspense films ever produced.

It begins with the arrival of two figures from Earth's future. One is a literal death machine, sent back to our century to kill a woman *before* she can become the mother of an individual who will have a tremendous positive impact on the future. The other futuristic visitor is a man sent here to kill the terminator before the robot can kill the woman. The writer has immediately set up a basic situation of suspense. Will the hero find the robot in time to save the would-be victim? Who will live and who will die?

The suspense keeps increasing as the robot hunter gets closer and closer to his female target. We are shown his awesome strength and cold ferocity as he smashes and destroys anyone in his way.

The hero, our man from tomorrow, falls in love with the woman, and he now fights for her life on a *personal* level. He finds that the killer robot cannot be destroyed by bullets, explosion, or fire. Each of these action sequences proves the robot's invincibility anew, heightening the suspense.

At the climax of the film, the robot is trapped in a fire-blasted truck. All of its "human" flesh is burned away, yet it *keeps on* pursuing the heroine. The Terminator is a walking horror that seemingly *nothing* can stop.

With suspense at fever pitch, the heroine finally crushes the robot into metal mush in the powerful jaws of a factory stamping machine.

Ending the suspense — and ending the film.

Rent the video. Watch it on your VCR and make notes of how the story builds one layer of suspense over another to a screaming point. That's what you need to do with your horror novel. Your tale need not be as extreme as *The Terminator*, which was a tour de force in the genre, but you must make certain that your narrative contains the necessary elements of suspense that will draw your audience relentlessly toward the climax.

Finally, then, *suspense* is the pulse of life beneath the flesh of your story.

The tell-tale heart of horror.

6.
BUILDING YOUR HOUSE
OF HORRORS

I n this chapter, I'll be covering a variety of topics, including style, outlines, dialogue, sensory description, humor, and point of view. You
should look on these topics as building blocks, designed to help you in the
construction of your house of horrors. Each is important in building a
successful and effective horror tale, whether it be long or short. You're the
final architect, but I can help you with the floor plan.

Let's begin by talking about the formation of a writer's style — the special
subjects, the individual approach, characteristic of that writer alone. When
you read a story by Ray Bradbury or Ernest Hemingway or H.P. Lovecraft
or Norman Mailer, there is an immediate recognition that this work is
special, unique, that the writer has placed a strong brand on the work. A
personal trademark.

How does this apply to you? How do you find *your* true voice, *your*
characteristic concerns?

I've been asked how long it took me to develop my own writing style.
How hard have I worked on it? The truth is, I've *never* worked on it. My
style emerged naturally from countless hours of writing.

Style is not some mysterious, arcane process that must be analyzed and
labored over; it is no more than the individual voice of the writer finding
its way to paper. You may have to write a great deal in order to develop
that personal voice. Most beginning writers, uncertain of their talent, at
first imitate role models. I imitated Ray Bradbury in the early days (his
masterful collection, *Dark Carnival*, was a tremendous influence); today,
most young horror writers imitate Stephen King.

But editors are not going to buy imitations of King or Bradbury or anybody else. You can learn many things as you imitate an admired popular

writer, but the more you write, the quicker you'll be able to shed the influences — and the easier it will be to find your own voice.

You can't force it. You cannot *impose* a style on your work. Style is the natural extension of a writer's personality. Having been nurtured on films, art, comic books, and early TV, my prose tends to be highly visual. (I could *see* Logan running inside my head long before MGM put him on the screen.) I try for direct clarity, a narrative with no wasted words, which communicates what I wish to say without frills or flourishes, writer to reader. That's what we're all doing, all writers: attempting to communicate directly with our audience. Anything that gets in the way of that line of communication should be eliminated.

The Well of Self

How we write is strongly influenced by *what* we write about. Style grows out of our roots, which is why we should value and cherish the memories of our childhood years; it is this seedbed that we will be dipping into and drawing upon all our adult lives as writers. What if your childhood was miserable? Can you use it as a writer?

Absolutely. The factors that caused your misery have dramatic value; use them to deepen your work. Too many writers do everything in their power to get away from their roots; they leave their hometown and emotionally turn their backs on it. Then they try to find new roots — and discover they can't. They attempt to ignore their past and forge a false future — then wonder why it is that they have nothing *real* to write about. The town they grew up in is a bore to them, and they stubbornly avoid writing about it or the people they knew in that town. All of which is self-defeating and counterproductive, since we must always write out of *ourselves*. (I call it "dipping into the well of self.")

Let me cite an example. During his early years as a writer, Bradbury had a rough time selling his work. Editors found his detective stories and fantasy fiction to be unreal, falsified, faked. He wasn't being true to his emotional self. Then one afternoon he sat down at his typewriter and turned out "The Lake." It was a story drawn from the deep emotional core of his childhood — and with it he had suddenly found his style, his own personal voice, which grew out of his boyhood in Illinois.

Stephen King writes mostly about people and things in the state of Maine. Why? Because that's his home; his emotional roots are there.

Half of my horror fiction deals with Missouri life and Missouri people; the other half is based in Southern California (the greater Los Angeles area). Why is so much of my work concentrated in these two areas? Because I *know* them. I spent my early years in Kansas City and my adult years in Los Angeles. When I write about these places and these people, my work rings true. It is authentic.

So don't discard your childhood. Meld it to your adulthood. And while that hometown of yours may be dull to you, it will be fresh and new to your readers; they'll be seeing it for the first time through *your* words. And the voice you speak with, on the page, is the style you've been seeking.

Finding your style is simply a matter of finding yourself.

The Bare Bones: That Essential Outline

Beginning writers are often confused about outlines for novels. Do you need them? How long should they be? How detailed? Should you outline each chapter?

Eventually, you will have to answer all these questions for yourself. Outlines tend to be extremely flexible; they differ in approach, length, and plot detail.

Some writers don't use outlines at all. These writers, though, have usually been around the track many times; their editors trust them to produce fully professional work each time out. A phone call or an idea hastily scribbled on a note pad may generate a book contract for these authors.

You, on the other hand, *do* need to provide an outline on your novel. There are two reasons. An outline helps you through the long process of writing the novel; it provides a road map so you won't get lost. An outline also proves to an editor that you know what you're going to be writing about. No editor is going to buy a book from a beginner unless that editor is convinced the writer has a full grasp of his or her plot and characters.

If you're not submitting a completed manuscript, you are going to have to send the first three chapters, along with an outline for the rest of the book. This is to show the editor that you can actually produce professional prose—and to demonstrate your pace and direction.

The outline for the remainder of the novel can be as complete as you wish to make it. At the least, it should take the editor through the entire plot, showing the main dramatic structure you'll be following, right into your ending. You must show the editor what becomes of your characters, and you must resolve the story.

How you do this is your concern. Some outlines, such as the one Stephen King and Peter Straub prepared for their joint novel, *The Talisman*, are extremely detailed and contain dialogue, miniscenes, and a chapter-by-chapter breakdown of the book's action.

This really isn't necessary. So long as you provide the editor with your basic plot and characters, he or she will be satisfied. You can do this in twenty or thirty typed pages (beyond your completed three chapters, that is).

In the outline itself, you need not use dialogue; it can be a straightforward nuts-and-bolts summary of what the book will contain and where it will go.

I begin my outlines with unlined 4″ × 6″ cards, on which I jot down characters, scenes, ideas, and plot fragments. Then I spread them on the floor, arranging them in the rough order of the basic plotline. I add new cards as new thoughts come to me. I try not to shortcut spontaneous creativity. My finished outline is never more than a basic guide to the novel itself; I don't bind myself to the outline, because for me, the best part of writing a novel is surprising myself with scenes, sequences, and characters that emerge from the narrative as I write.

Whatever your individual outline method, just remember to stay flexible. Give your subconscious a chance to be heard, and you'll be amazed at what pops up.

The Functions of Dialogue

One of the most important building blocks in horror is effective dialogue.

Dialogue sets mood, delineates character, moves the story forward, clarifies plot points, and reveals the emotional levels of your characters.

Dialogue can also establish tension. As in Hemingway's terse classic, "The Killers":

> "We're going to kill a Swede. Do you know a big Swede named Ole Andreson?"
> "Yes."
> "He comes here to eat every night, don't he?"

"Sometimes he comes here."

"He comes here at six o'clock, don't he?"

*"If he comes . . . What are you going to kill Ole Andreson for?
What did he ever do to you?"*

*"He never had a chance to do anything to us. He never even seen
us."*

"And he's only going to see us once," Al said.

The principles of writing effective dialogue apply to all fiction, not just to
the horror field. All good dialogue is both artificial and deceptive. No one
ever spoke as tersely or as clipped as a Hemingway character, or as lyrically
as a Fitzgerald heroine, or as tough and mannered as a Chandler detective.
Most dialogue is far removed from what people really say to each other,
yet good fictional dialogue should *sound* like actual conversation. Sit down
at the counter of a crowded coffee shop and *listen* to the conversations
going on around you. The talkers ramble. They stray from the point. They
are repetitive, shallow, and often boring. A great many words are used to
say very little.

As a writer, you must accomplish certain things with your dialogue.
Dialogue must keep your novel or story moving along its track; it must
advance, not halt, the narrative. Your dialogue should reveal character—
sometimes in very subtle, understated ways, and sometimes (as the scene
demands) in blunt, explosively dramatic terms. And what your people say
to each other should tell readers things they need to know about the plot.

In my story "Something Nasty," I use dialogue to establish a past relationship between an evil uncle and his niece, as well as characterizing the
man as a sponger:

"Why are you crying?"

"Because," said Janey.

"Because why?"

"Because I don't want to talk to Uncle Gus."

"But he adores *you! He comes over especially to see you."*

*"No, he doesn't," said Janey . . . "He doesn't adore me and he
doesn't come specially to see me. He comes to get money from Daddy."*

Her mother was shocked. "That's a terrible thing to say!"

"But it's true. Isn't it true?"

"Your Uncle Gus was hurt in the war. He can't hold down an ordinary job. We just do what we can to help him."

"He never liked me," said Janey.

Thus, always: Dialogue is *action.*

It must be far more compressed than real-life dialogue, and it must contain shades of meaning. You have ground to cover in a dialogue sequence, points to make, truths to reveal. Under the mask of realistic conversation, these things must be accomplished.

The Menacing Tone in Horror

What about dialogue in a horror story? How does it differ from the dialogue used in other forms of fiction? For one thing, it often acquires a sinister, below-surface sense of menace, of threat, of danger.

Consider Bradbury's dialogue exchange in "The Wind":

The phone rang at six-thirty that evening. It was December, and already dark as Thompson picked up the phone.

"Hello."

"Hello, Herb?"

"Oh, it's you, Allin."

"Is your wife home, Herb?"

"Sure. Why?"

"Damn it."

Herb Thompson held the receiver quietly. "What's up? You sound funny."

"I wanted you to come over tonight."

"We're having company." . . .

"I wish you could come over tonight."

"Wish I could. Company and all. My wife'd kill me."

"I wish you could come over."

"What's it—the wind again?"

"Oh, no. No."

"Is it the wind?" asked Thompson.

The voice on the phone hesitated. "Yeah. Yeah, it's the wind."

Here's another example of promised menace, from Philip Dick's "The Father-Thing":

> "He's the other one," Charles muttered, face white, hands beginning to tremble. Suddenly he leaped up and backed away from the dinner table. "Get away!" he shouted. "Get out of [our house]!"
>
> "Hey," Ted rumbled ominously. "What's got into you? . . . You sit down there and eat your dinner, young man. Your mother didn't fix it for nothing."
>
> Charles turned and ran out of the kitchen . . .
>
> Ted went on eating. His face was grim; his eyes were hard and dark. "That kid," he grated, "is going to have to learn a few things. Maybe he and I need to have a little private conference together."

"Better to See You With, My Dear"

Each reader has a nose, ears, eyes, a tongue to taste with, fingers to touch with, and skin that registers external stimuli such as heat and cold. Full descriptive use of these senses in your fiction will subtly influence the reader; he or she will become far more involved in your story if the scenes you write contain direct sensory impressions. Your work will achieve greater depth and physical immediacy.

When your character enters a room for the first time, it's up to you to provide the reader with the vision of all the relevant objects in that room. You need not *over*-describe. However, you must show whatever is necessary to convey mood, or information, or viewpoint. The same holds true for clothing and terrain. Not *everything* need be described (God forbid!), but the things that count dramatically have to be brought to life before the eyes of your audience. Remember, the reader starts out blind; the reader sees only through your eyes. You are the artist; you paint the scene with your words.

What your character *hears* also adds to the total sensory picture. The patter of rain on the roof . . . the ticking of a clock . . . the howl of a dog in the distance . . . the sudden blare of a car horn . . . the menacing click of a cocked revolver . . . all such details help you build the proper atmosphere for your terror tale.

The sense of *touch* is often overlooked. Yet this subtle element adds greatly to your narrative if properly utilized.

To demonstrate the difference between a nonsensory approach and a sensory approach:

Non-sensory:

He was nervous as he held the automatic.

Sensory:

His palm was moist *as it pressed into the cold handle of the automatic.*

The sensory image of the character's sweating palm against the cool gun gives us the same information as the first sentence (he was nervous), but it is much more involving for the reader, who is now able to *feel* the gun, just as your character does.

Incorporating the senses of *smell* and *taste* can also strongly affect your reader. Blood has an *odor:* let your character smell it as she enters the room. Dead skin does not feel the same as living skin. Let him touch the dead girl's face and feel the chilled texture of the skin. Fear puts a rusty taste in the mouth. Don't just tell your reader that your protagonist is afraid: let the sensory *taste* of it become a part of your scene.

These elements are all valuable tools in the construction of horror; they should be used as a carpenter uses the proper hammers, chisels, and saws. Make yourself proficient in the employment of the senses; they are essential to your craft. They need not *all* be employed in the same scene, but they should be ready in your mind, and you should always be aware of their potential in your work.

Scared Silly

Horror fiction, like cooked meat, often needs a bit of seasoning, and even though most readers would never consciously link humor and horror, the two can often be combined to excellent effect. Don't be afraid to stir a bit of humor into your suspense-terror mix. It can serve as a relief valve, offering the reader a chance to ease back from the unrelenting intensity of the narrative. But be warned: Unless the writer deliberately sets out to tell a rib-tickling story, humor must be used with discretion. In a serious suspense tale, you must never outweigh horror with humor.

Bestselling novelist Dean Koontz can be a very funny man on paper (the newsletters he wrote for the Horror Writers of America were hilarious), but when he's into a shock novel, he reins in much of his natural humor to create his horrific scenes. Still, the seasoning is there, as in the Koontz novel *Midnight*:

> "*I underwent a near-death experience. . . . Rose out of my body, drifted up to the ceiling, watched the surgeons for awhile, then found myself rushing faster and faster down a dark tunnel toward this dazzling light — the whole screwy scenario.*"
>
> "*And?*"
>
> "*I saw what lies beyond.*" . . .
>
> "*Well? Don't keep me hanging. What'd you see on the other side?*"
>
> "*If I tell you, you'll think I'm crazy.*"
>
> "*You've got nothing to lose. I already think you're crazy.*"

Humor is used much more broadly in horror films — such as the constant wisecracking of Freddy in the *Nightmare on Elm Street* series — but that's because a viewing audience tends to scream *and* giggle during a horror movie. It's part of the fun. A reader sitting alone after midnight with a horror novel is not looking for laughs.

Point of View

Beginning writers are often confused about whether they should write in the first, second, or third person, as well as how they should structure the character's point of view.

In a hard-boiled private eye story, a first-person narrative is accepted and traditional. The detective personally guides readers through the adventure, sharing each moment of love and danger with them, winding things up with the final solution of the case.

In horror fiction, a first-person narrative can prove to be troublesome; the writer must be more careful in its use. For one thing, sometimes the taleteller, as victim of the evil he or she combats, does not survive the narrative. (This has been the case in many short stories.) Even if he or she does survive, and tells the story first person, the reader can never be sure *how* and *to whom* the story is being told.

With my first-person "Fair Trade," I solved this dilemma by having the protagonist record his version of the grisly proceedings on an audio tape cassette at the request of the sheriff. And in another of my shorter works, "The Cure," I had him put his thoughts and actions down in a notebook:

> *Maybe after I'm dead somebody will find this notebook and read what I say and if they do I guess they'll judge me as some kind of crazy man who goes around killing innocent people.*

The advantage of a first-person approach is that it does provide a special intimacy between narrator and reader, which in certain types of stories can be very effective. I personally like to use it in my folksy horror, in which the narrator is a good ole boy who rambles on in an easygoing manner. This tends to disarm the reader, making the character warm and likable. (I use this approach in my story "The Partnership.") At the point I allow the character to reveal his evil side, the shock is all the greater.

From the story's early section (establishing warmth):

> *Me and Sally kid each other a lot, but we're both too old to have it mean anything. But she likes me. Most folks do. And that's nice. Person wants to know he's liked.*

From the story's closing section (revealing evil):

> *The bearded stranger was already dead . . . and most of his head was gone, but Ed had been careful not to muss up his clothes—so I had no problem getting his wallet, rings, cash. . . .*

For most horror fiction, however, I feel that a third-person approach (use *he* or *she*, not *I*) works best. When the horror is about to engulf the protagonist, the author can stand back and describe the action with a degree of detached irony, as I did in the ending of my story "Ceremony":

*. . . rubbery tubes. Coiling out from his body into the figures sur-
rounding him, a tube for each of them, attached to his flesh and ending
in their flesh — like obscene umbilical cords.*

I think the third-person narrative is easier to handle for a beginning writer,
and in an overall reader sense, I think it is usually more convincing. As
you gain skill and confidence, you can try some first-person narratives.

A second-person narrative approach (the viewpoint character is referred
to as *you*) is almost never used. The form is awkward and calls undue
attention to itself. (Similarly, mood music in films deepens and enhances
the drama, but needs to remain subliminal. If viewers become *aware* of the
musical scoring, they also become outside spectators rather than involved
participants in the unfolding story.)

Very occasionally, a second-person narrative *can* be effective, as in Bradbury's urban horror tale "A Careful Man Dies":

*You sleep only four hours a night. You go to bed at eleven and get
up at three. . . . You begin your day then, have your coffee, read a book
for an hour, listen to the faint, far, unreal music of the pre-dawn sta-
tions, and perhaps you go out for a walk. . . . this is how your life goes.*

In the classic and seminal Japanese film *Rashomon*, an important dramatic event is presented from several viewpoints. Each character has seen
this same violent event from a personal perspective, and each reports it
differently.

Point of view is present in nearly every scene of every story and novel.
Purely objective writing (see Dashiell Hammett's *The Glass Key*), in which
the author never reveals the inner thoughts and emotions of the characters, is rare indeed. It keeps the reader at too great a distance. An objective
approach is not appropriate in horror writing, since emotion and sensory
detail are needed to build and maintain suspense.

Therefore, assuming your scene *will* have a definite point of view, how
do you decide which character's point of view should be adopted?

Most of your story should be presented from the viewpoint of your
protagonist. He or she naturally dominates the action, and the reader iden-
tifies most strongly with this central character. However, it is often useful
(particularly in novels) to present alternating viewpoints, chapter to chapter. This allows a change of tone and mood, and it also allows you to

provide a high degree of cliffhanging suspense. (At the end of chapter five in your book, the hero is just about to open a Very Terrible Door—and you jump away from him into chapter six, as another character carries the narrative football for a chapter or two.)

Study the novels of Dean Koontz for a masterful application of this technique. He sets up a group of perhaps four or five characters (one of which is his protagonist) and allows the reader to follow each of them in various alternating chapters. As they get into serious danger he cuts away to another character, returning to the first character's hazardous situation in a later chapter—cleverly moving his various characters along his narrative board like pieces in a chess game.

Koontz's *Midnight* offers a superb example of what I'm talking about. No wonder this horror novel was such a smash best seller; the events keep you on the edge of your chair throughout the book, first page to last.

Let me warn you: In a short story, due to its brevity, such constant switching is not advised. Most short stories are told from a single viewpoint—that of the protagonist.

And unless you are after a special shock effect, *never* switch viewpoints within a scene. To have the narrative viewpoint change in the middle of an ongoing sequence is very jarring to the reader. If you *must* switch, wait until the scene has ended.

Matching Tone with Character

Viewpoint varies greatly depending on a character's age, sex, background, etc. A child has one viewpoint, a mother another, an elderly man yet another.

As the author, it's up to you to set a correct tone with whatever character dominates the sequence.

Almost all of Bradbury's *Dandelion Wine* is told from the viewpoint of a young boy, Doug, who is just on the verge of entering his teenage years. Thus, the observations, the descriptions, and the dialogue are all filtered through Doug's mind and given in his wording. We see that special Illinois summer through *his* eyes. The adolescent tone is carefully maintained and controlled throughout.

When I wrote "Fair Trade," I chose to make my main character an ignorant illiterate. Therefore, his version of events and his observations are crude and basic, in keeping with his particular point of view:

I don't recall I ever had no blood kinfolk — 'cept my Ma and my Pappy an' I never knew 'em proper. Not enough to hang a recollection on 'em. They both took off when I was a tad an' left me . . . an' I run away an' just growed as best I could, livin' off the woods and what you find there.

I've been writing fiction for more than thirty-five years, and with each of my stories and novels I make a choice as to what character will dominate a particular story or chapter.

It's a great joy — bringing new characters to life on a page.

And your writing, if well done, should always be a joy.

7.
PLANTING THE HOOK

I n 1963, when I was editor of *Gamma*, a West Coast fantasy publication, I spent one day each week reading from the *slush pile* (unagented manuscripts submitted by beginning writers). I was looking for stories good enough to print in the magazine, but there was a strict rule I followed: If the opening paragraphs of the story didn't grab me, I quit reading after that first page. An automatic rejection. This may have seemed unfair to some of those beginning writers, but I felt at that time (as I do now) that a story (or novel) must grab its audience immediately with an arresting image or with fresh dialogue or with an intriguing situation that promises forthcoming thrills and chills.

Grabbing Your Reader

So how do you hook your reader?

The best way for me to answer this is by quoting opening sections from a variety of horror stories and novels. Study these examples. Think about them. Analyze their content. Ask yourself, with each: What makes me want to go on reading? What has the author done to plant the narrative hook?

> *No live organism can continue for long to exist sanely under conditions of absolute reality; even larks and katydids are supposed, by some, to dream. Hill House, not sane, stood by itself against its hills, holding darkness within; it had stood so for eighty years and might stand for eighty more. Within, walls continued upright, bricks met neatly, floors were firm, and doors were sensibly shut; silence lay stead-*

ily against the wood and stone of Hill House, and whatever walked there, walked alone.

—*from* The Haunting of Hill House, *by Shirley Jackson*

This day when it had light mother called me retch. You retch she said. I saw in her eyes the anger. I wonder what it is a retch.

—*from "Born of Man and Woman," by Richard Matheson*

Maybe most of it was only fear. But not the last thing, not that. To blame my fear for that would be worst of all.

—*from"The Chimney," by Ramsey Campbell*

This morning I put ground glass in my wife's eyes. She didn't mind. She didn't make a sound. She never does.

—*from "The Dead Line," by Dennis Etchison*

He kept walking. The day was hot and miserable and he wiped his forehead. Up another twenty feet, he could make out more. Thank God. Maybe he'd find it all. He picked up the pace and his breathing got thick. He struggled on, remembering his vow to himself to go through with this, not stopping until he was done. Maybe it had been a mistake to ask this favor. But it was the only way he could think of to work it out. Still, maybe it had been a mistake.

—*from "Red," by Richard Christian Matheson*

They were from Indianapolis. Newly married. Dave and stirring, flexing muscle, feeling power now . . . anger . . . a sudden driving thirst for *Alice Williamson, both in their late twenties, both excited about their trip to the West Coast. This would be their last night in Arizona. Tomorrow they planned to be in Palm Springs. To visit Dave's sister. But only one of them would make it to California. Dave, not Alice.* with the scalpel glittering

Alice would die before midnight, her throat slashed cleanly across.

—*from "The Final Stone," by William F. Nolan*

What was the worst thing you've ever done?

I won't tell you that, but I'll tell you the worst thing that ever happened to me . . . the most dreadful thing.

—from Ghost Story, *by Peter Straub*

Midnight. Black as the heart of Satan.

They came rolling out of the darkness in a black, '66 Chevy; eating up Highway 59 North like so much juicy, grey taffy. In the thickness of night, the car, all by its lonesome out there, seemed like a time machine from an evil future. Its lights were gold scalpels ripping apart the delicate womb of night, pushing forward through the viscera and allowing it to heal tightly behind it. The engine, smoothly tuned and souped-up heavy, moaned with sadistic pleasure.

—from The Nightrunners, *by Joe R. Lansdale*

When consciousness at last returned to Colin, it came in a rush to life so fast that agony itself wasn't instantly identifiable but a bewilderment which, instinctively, he knew was portentous. A sheer, evil omen. He found that he was crumpled at the bottom of a steep, damp shaft plunging down into the broken earth. Although he did not know how he'd gotten there, the fact that he didn't wonder about it was less the product of confusion than young Colin's nature. He'd always been pragmatic; an accepter, an adjuster.

—from "The House of Life," by J.N. Williamson

"That's the man, right over there," said Mrs. Ribmoll, nodding across the street. "See that man perched on the tar barrel afront Mr. Jenkins' store? Well, that's him. They call him Odd Martin."

—from "The Dead Man," by Ray Bradbury

The lashed-together framework of sticks jutted from a small cairn alongside the stream. Colin Leverett studied it in perplexment—half a dozen odd lengths of branch, wired together at cross angles for no fathomable purpose. It reminded him unpleasantly of some bizarre crucifix, and he wondered what might lie beneath the cairn.

—from "Sticks," by Karl Edward Wagner

There are only fragments of me left now. Chunks of memory have broken free and drifted away like calved glaciers. It is always like that when a Passenger leaves us.

—from "Passengers," by Robert Silverberg

It was 3:00 a.m., the dead, silent middle of the night. Except for the humming of the soft-drink machine in one corner, and the irregular, rumbling cough of the ice machine hidden in an alcove just beyond it, the lobby was quiet. There weren't likely to be any more check-ins until after dawn—all the weary cross-country drivers would be settled elsewhere by now, or grimly determined to push on without a rest.

—from "Sun City," by Lisa Tuttle

David Lashley huddled the skimpy blankets around him and dully watched the cold light of morning seep through the window and stiffen in his room. He could not recall the exact nature of the terror against which he had fought his way to wakefulness, except that it had been in some way gigantic, and had brought back to him the fear-ridden helplessness of childhood. It had lurked near him all night and finally it had crouched over him and thrust down toward his face.

—from "The Hound," by Fritz Leiber

With many stories and novels, the opening sentence alone can hook the reader instantly.

"The Reach was wider in those days," Stella Flanders told her great-grandchildren in the last summer of her life, the summer before she began to see ghosts.

—from "The Reach," by Stephen King

As Gregor Samsa awoke one morning from uneasy dreams he found himself transformed in his bed into a gigantic insect.

—from "The Metamorphosis," by Franz Kafka

"Now then," said the psychiatrist, looking up from his note pad, "when did you first discover that you were dead?"

—from "Blood Brother," by Charles Beaumont

64

A storm struck on the night Laura Shane was born, and there was a strangeness about the weather that people would remember for years.

—from Lightning, *by Dean R. Koontz*

When a traveller in north central Massachusetts takes the wrong fork at the junction of the Aylesbury pike just beyond Dean's Corners he comes upon a lonely and curious country.

—from "The Dunwich Horror," by H.P. Lovecraft

I was lying on the floor watching TV and exercising what was left of my legs when the newscaster's jaw collapsed.

—from "Soft," by F. Paul Wilson

Tonight there were demons in the hearth.

—from They Thirst, *by Robert R. McCammon*

"They say," said the Countess, absently fondling the brooch at her young throat, "that he's the devil."

—from "The Cage," by Ray Russell

Such one-liners *compel* a reader to continue; they tease and tantalize, promising unique delights.

In each story, at the outset, the reader should become aware that something is amiss, that a threat is hanging over the characters, that danger, in some form, is waiting at the edge of the horizon. In this way, the reader is drawn immediately into the narrative; curiosity is aroused. A promise has been given, from author to reader: If you want to be frightened, I'll provide a fright; all you have to do is stick with me.

All this comes out of your opening. The sooner the reader is made aware of an impending terror, the quicker he or she will be locked into your story. We live in a fast-paced world; readers are easily bored. If you don't provide what they are seeking in the opening section of a horror story, they'll give up and go elsewhere for their thrills.

A Gripping Exercise

I suggest that you pick up one of the anthologies that I have listed in the Appendix—ideally *The Arbor House Treasury of Horror and the Supernatural*. This volume contains forty-one stories. Read *only the opening page* of each story in the book, then write down what elements are contained in those first pages. Study them. *Learn* from them. You'll see how each story in the collection wastes no time in taking the reader aboard for its voyage into terror.

And once you've learned how to plant your hook, you'll be prepared to go fishing.

For readers.

8.
MASKS, SHADOWS, AND SURPRISES

Horror fiction is full of symbols.

Evil. Good. The Devil. God. The Universe. Salvation. Eternity.

Therefore, it's important that a new writer learn how to get these symbols into the story, right?

No. I don't happen to think so.

When people ask me about the symbolic meaning of this or that particular object in a story of mine, my answer is always the same. I tell them, "Read into it what you will."

Hemingway once got very peeved with a review of his novel *Across the River and Into the Trees* when the critic pointed out that the white bird that flies out of the gondola during a romantic moment symbolized the loss of the heroine's virginity.

"That white bird was just something I wrote into the scene because I thought it was a nice touch," declared Hemingway. "It sure as hell wasn't anybody's flying virginity."

Of course, the author had every right to be peeved, and, conversely, the critic had every right to find whatever symbols he felt were contained in Hemingway's writing.

The point I'm making here is that you shouldn't *consciously* place symbols in your work, because such implants often create an awkward, artificial impression. It's impossible for any of us to write fiction without automatically inserting hidden symbolism on various levels. Our subconscious minds will do this for us, so we need not worry ourselves over this aspect of writing. Symbolism properly flows from the subconscious and becomes a natural part of the narrative. Allow your readers to discover whatever symbolism they perceive. Whatever interpretation a reader chooses to make of your work should be of no concern to you.

Paradoxically, by *consciously* ignoring symbolism, you will allow your subconscious mind to work freely; you will then discover that symbolism will indeed be an integral — and important — part of your writing.

Basement-Level Fears

An effective horror tale should leave the reader with something to think about after the final page, something beyond what is revealed on the surface; the story should resonate within the reader's psyche. Therefore, I often construct a kind of subconscious, basement level beneath the main floor of my narrative. It has to do with the primitive in each of us.

To frighten a reader at a very deep level, you have to be able to tap into primal fears, and these fears are always buried below the conscious. For example, in my story "The Halloween Man," a young schoolgirl becomes obsessed with a ghoul-creature, a stealer of souls, who, it is said, appears only on Halloween night. She convinces herself that he's real, and when her father, at the story's climax, attempts to calm her fears, she is suddenly sure that *he's* the Halloween Man. But is he? Or is it all in her mind? The reader is left to ponder the creature's ultimate reality. Thus, I achieve an echo effect. Many of my stories are constructed on this double level: reality versus illusion.

The character in my "Fair Trade" tells the sheriff about a grisly murder. But he says *he* didn't do it. He simply followed a newly risen corpse into town and watched the dead man commit the murder. Tells about the whole experience in vivid detail. Is his statement to the sheriff the product of a deranged mind, or did the horror take place as he described it? I leave my readers to answer this for themselves.

Over the Edge

I've always been fascinated by dramatizing the emotionally charged edge between sanity and madness. A number of my horror stories concern characters who are about to go over this edge. How do they deal with the inner pressures that have driven them toward madness?

Nothing in this world of ours can match the self-imposed terrors of the human mind. It's the fiend in all of us. Insanity is a dream from which a person cannot wake; in the mind, *any* horror is possible. If you are in the backyard taking out the trash and your mind tells you there is a scorpion as large as a Ford truck near the fence, you'll believe it's there. Your wife may say you're crazy, but you'll give her a spirited argument, once your mind has convinced you that the thing is out there. And she'll never be able to share *your* reality.

Thus, distortions in the human mind offer a horror writer endless possibilities. That's one reason, among many, that I have always avoided drugs; I don't want to alter the chemical balance of my brain. As a writer, my brain is all I've got. (And what's in there is bad enough already!)

A Delightful Shock

Readers enjoy being surprised, perhaps more so in horror fiction than in other genres. They want to *think* they know what's coming next, but when you jar them in a whole new direction, they delight in being thrown off-balance. Sometimes the misdirection is slight; other times it can be a total shock. In my "Saturday's Shadow," I allow readers to assume that the protagonist we are following through the story is a woman, the mentally unstable sister of the tough cop described in the narrative. Only at the climax do I reveal that it is the *cop* who's been center-stage from the beginning, that *he's* the crazy one, unsure of his own identity. He ends by shooting his sister to save her from the imagined evil of Saturday's Shadow. Here is a total twist in character that shocks and surprises.

In a more recent story, "Him, Her, Them," I again misdirect my readers, leading them to believe that the "Him" in the early part of the story is a psycho killer. When the woman he brings home actually ends up killing him, we realize that *she* is the psycho. Once my readers settle into the belief that they are reading about this *same* woman in the second part of the story, "Her," I have the woman murdered by *another* man, revealing her to have been a totally different character. In "Them," at the climax of the story, I bring the two original killers together, each planning to eliminate the other. Thus, my entire narrative is one of deliberate misdirection; each section of the story delivers its own shock-surprise.

I do this again in "The Yard." Told in first person, it deals with a protagonist who returns to his hometown for his father's funeral. There's an evil junkyard owner in the town whose one-eyed dog keeps a highway watch for potential crash victims who can be hauled back to the yard and devoured. At the end, I create a horrific scene in which the dog rips savagely at the protagonist's flesh, obviously killing him. (Yet the story is being told in first person!) After a space, I resume with:

> *I felt the need to move. To leave the Yard. The air was cold, edged with the promise of frost. The sky was steel gray above me.*
>
> *It was good to move again. To run. To leave the town and the woods behind me.*
>
> *It was very quiet. I gloried in the strong scent of earth and metal which surrounded me. I was alive. And strong again. It was fine to be alive.*
>
> *I waited. Occasionally a shape passed in front of me, moving rapidly. I ignored it. Another. And another. And then, finally, the one. Happiness rushed through me. Here was one who would provide my life and strength and the life and strength of my master.*
>
> *I raised my head. He saw me then, the one in the truck. My eye fixed on his as he swept past me with a metallic rush of sound. And vanished into the fog.*
>
> *I sat quietly, waiting for the crash.*

Thus, the reader is shocked to discover that the protagonist is now alive *within* the body of the dog. The creature has claimed his soul.

Don't be afraid to misdirect your readers. You'll be taking them places they never expected to reach—and they'll love you for it.

This Line of Work May Prove Frightening

Do horror writers actually frighten themselves as they write? You bet they do. It's happened to me several times—and at those moments, you know that you have created a particularly scary sequence.

Some writers use self-fright as a working concept. Novelist-editor Charles L. Grant, one of the genre's most active talents, admits that he will not write about a subject that doesn't frighten him. "Everything I write frightens me," says Grant. "I don't send a story out unless I'm scared at the end, unless I get that chill. . . ."

Another very successful practitioner in the genre, Michael McDowell, also admits he's easily frightened. "What often affects me as I'm working are childhood fears, specific things from my boyhood. When I was writing

'The Elementals,' I was working until two o'clock every night upstairs in my study. I remember having to stop because I was so shaken . . . having written things that really frightened me."

Self-fright is, therefore, a common experience among horror writers; it means that we are digging into primal areas, stirring up deeply buried fears, bringing them onto the page in a very intense and concentrated way.

For our genre, this is a plus. It's always good to become emotionally involved with what you are writing. The more involved you are, the more involved your readers will be. Hack writers merely skim the surface of their subjects, but the authors that readers return to again and again are emotionally committed to the material they create.

Some years ago, I was writing the outline for a television horror movie. I was in an all-night coffee shop, sitting at the end of the counter, writing in a tablet with my felt-tip pen. It was very late, and I was alone at the counter. The waitress was having her break, and the place was dead silent. I was writing about a really Awful Creature on the loose, creeping about the brush-covered hills of the San Fernando Valley in Los Angeles, searching for human victims. Two young women (Ellen and Mish) are playing a game of night tennis on a hillside court, which is bounded by a chain-link fence covered with green canvas. The ball is knocked over the fence into the lower brush and Ellen goes after it. Here's the rest of the scene I wrote that night:

> CAMERA is with Ellen in the bushes when, suddenly, above her, all the overhead lights go out. Now the only illumination is provided by a row of dim green bulbs spaced at ten-foot intervals along the exit passage between the fenced courts. Their green glow is ominous.
>
> "I can't see a bloody thing down here," Ellen yells.
>
> We are now back on the shadowed court with Mish, who is gathering up their tennis gear. She calls down to her friend: "Just forget that dumb ball. It's time to head home, okay?"
>
> But there is no reply from the dark mass of tangled brush on the hillside.
>
> "Elly . . . Ellen! . . . Answer me, you goon!"
>
> She walks to the fence, peers downward.
>
> No sound. No movement. Just the mournful dirge of night crickets.
>
> Mish is getting nervous. She calls Ellen's name again — without a

reply. Mish stands tensely at the cold metal fence, her eyes probing the gray-green dimness.

Then, loud and piercing, a SCREAM OF TERROR from the hill. Ellen's scream. The sound is abruptly cut off — and there is only silence again.

Then, a rustle of movement. The soft crackle of brush . . .

Mish can hardly allow herself to breathe; terror fills her body, shines from her round eyes as she sees:

A pair of rotted, mud-clotted feet, half-bone, half-flesh, visible in the shadows under the stretched green canvas — moving toward her along the fence on the opposite side.

Mish jerks back, pushing a knuckled hand into her mouth, biting flesh to stifle the sounds in her throat. Her eyes shift to:

The court gate.

It stands open where Ellen left it.

Mish suddenly breaks for the gate — but just as she reaches it the fence canvas in front of her is ripped aside with tremendous force — and we see (CAMERA ZOOMING IN) a demented face that is older than that of any human being. Not 100 . . . Not 150 . . . but vastly older.

With a strangled sob, Mish plunges through the gate, runs wildly along the exit passage under the glowing green bulbs, half-falls, drags herself up, plunges forward, gasping, out of her senses with fear.

The creature behind her moves fast, rapidly closing the space between them. Rotted bits of flesh fall from its body as it pursues her, and it is brandishing what seems to be a club . . .

Mish reaches the parking lot. Jumps into her car. Fumbles in her purse for keys. Can't find them. The creature is almost to the car. She rolls up the window and the creature's rotted hands scrabble at the glass. He batters the window with his club . . . Mish finally locates the ignition key. Stabs it into the dash. Engine ROARS. She punches the gas. Too much — as the car whips around in a tire-churning circle. The engine dies. The creature continues to batter at the window, smashing the glass. Mish grinds the starter; the engine fires up again. She floors the pedal, blasting away in a spume of gravel.

We see the car fishtailing down the court road.

We HEAR the soft CRUNCHING of pebbles as the creature moves forward CLOSE INTO FRAME. His back is to us, but his hunched figure

FILLS THE SCREEN as he watches the taillights of the car fade into the darkness.

We HEAR the wet, bubbly SOUND of the creature's breathing.

CAMERA SLOWLY PANS DOWN to his hand, in which he still holds the club.

But it is not a club.

It is Ellen's left arm.

When I wrote that last line I actually had goosebumps, and my heart was pounding. I had *experienced* the fear as I was writing the scene. The emotion was genuine. I'd achieved true terror on the page.

Believe me, it's worth going for. It's what the genre is all about.

Revision: It Can Haunt You Too Soon

I want to caution you regarding first drafts. Don't tinker with them as they are being written. Don't stop in the middle to go back and rewrite earlier sections.

If you're writing a novel, and you come to a section you're not ready to write (for whatever reason), just skip on past it, leaving a note to yourself on the page:

Do more research. Or,

Develop characters. Or,

Insert scene in cemetery here.

Whatever applies. Then plunge on with the writing.

Never stop to revise.

Revision is the main reason for the countless unfinished manuscripts some writers accumulate. How many times have new writers told me: "I just can't seem to finish my novel. I keep getting bogged down every time I rewrite the early parts."

These writers have lost their focus. They can't see the woods for the trees. They're no longer writing out of creative passion, because they've lost the forward movement that is essential to the writing process.

Get the story down on paper and *then* worry about revising it. Go with the "heat" of a first draft. Go with your *emotions.* Later, when you have finished your story, you will have plenty of time to go back and intellectualize. You will be able to fix anything that needs fixing. You will be able to deepen and polish. To bring in new characters. To cut dead sections that slow down or impede the narrative flow.

Flow is the key word here. The basic flow of that first draft must not be interrupted. Nothing should slow your creative momentum. If you stop along the way for revisions, your book will likely never be completed. You'll get discouraged and abandon it. Your creative juices will have dried up, and instead of being fun to write, the book will become drudgery. So . . .

Finish that first draft.

Read, Read, and Read Some More

The path to writing is reading. It's the beginning for us all. All writers. Those early formative books we avidly devoured when we were young, those books that ignited the imagination and opened our minds, those books that (later) planted within us the delicious thought that we, too, might someday see stories of our own between covers.

The trouble with a great number of beginning writers—whether the field is Westerns, mysteries, romance, science fiction, heroic fantasy, or horror—is that they do not read beyond their genre. I have had writers tell me with pride that they have read every book by Stephen King. And all of Peter Straub. And now they're reading everything they can find by Dean Koontz.

"That's great," I say, "but have you read William Faulkner, John Steinbeck, F. Scott Fitzgerald, Norman Mailer, Truman Capote, Ernest Hemingway, John Cheever . . . ?"

They look at me blankly. Well, no. Not exactly. Of course, they've *heard* of all these authors—even sampled some of them in school—but they want to be *horror* writers, so now they read horror. What's wrong with that?

A lot. Knowing your field, reading all of the major writers within that field is to be expected, but if that's *all* you read, you are going to produce nothing more than pale imitations of other genre authors.

It is absolutely essential to read extensively *outside* the genre. It is this outside reading that will enable you to bring fresh perspective, insights, and attitudes to your chosen field.

I learned a tremendous amount about stretching the limits of fiction from reading William Faulkner's *The Sound and the Fury*. This novel, with its incredible, constant time shifts, past to present, present to past, proves how high a writer can climb on the tree of fiction, just how far out on the limb he can go.

Scott Fitzgerald taught me the value of rhythm in prose.

Steinbeck brought me vigor and local color.

Hemingway made me appreciate the terse, telling use of dialogue.

Hammett's *The Maltese Falcon* illuminated the objective prose technique.

Capote's *In Cold Blood* dramatized the key use of landscape in narrative.

Mailer taught me complex sentence structure.

James Thurber demonstrated the use of humor as a cutting edge in social commentary.

And from the Westerns of Max Brand, I learned how dramatic action can reveal character.

The list is endless. I could go on and name a hundred other writers who proved to be invaluable influences on my work down through the years.

Read the poetry of Robert Frost, the nature essays of Loren Eiseley, the plays of Tennessee Williams, the short stories of Eudora Welty, the parodies of S.J. Perelman, the hard-boiled novels of Raymond Chandler.

There's a big literary world out there, and as a writer, you can profit immeasurably from your journey beyond the genre. So . . .

Read!

Read!

Read!

9.
THE GORY DETAILS

Just how graphic should horror be?

It's not an easy question to answer. There are writers (myself included) who believe that less is more, that bloody acts of violence need not be graphically described or dramatized. As I stated in one of my columns in *Horrorstruck*:

> *My position is simple. I detest the Vomit Bag School of Horror, whether on screen or on the printed page—books and stories and films featuring gore for gore's sake, designed strictly for the purpose of grossing out an audience.*

In his preface to *Book of the Dead*, veteran horrormaster Robert Bloch has also spoken out against this form of entertainment:

> *Graphic gore [on the screen] and nauseating cruelty are substituted for true terror, and the basic audience appeal is to the legions of louts who revel in roller derbies. Taking their cues from this, many writers of horror fiction have sought to duplicate these visual excesses with the written word. . . . Soaked with sex and marinated in meaningless violence, some of this work succeeds on a fast-read level, but I strongly doubt if it will endure, or even be endurable to the sensibilities of readers in the decades ahead.*

Graphic horror cannot be ignored. It is most certainly a part of today's genre, and it has strong-voiced proponents. When the writing team of John Skipp and Craig Spector edited their graphic anthology, *Book of the Dead*, they declared themselves pioneers:

The function of the pioneer is to penetrate the unknown: to delve into those culturally uncharted places. . . . Despite the public outcry that it's time to stop, we've gone far enough, thank you — or perhaps, ironically, because of it — another handful of intrepid souls will feel the itch to probe a little deeper. To expand the horizon. To go too far.

How Far Is Too Far?

Thus, Skipp and Spector believe that the boundaries of the genre must be pushed to the ultimate, that writers must not flinch from the visceral depiction of the most graphic of bloody acts. Anything short of this is to stand still, to bury one's head in the sand, to avert one's eyes. In their view, it is *impossible* to go "too far."

Children constantly go too far. Indeed, going too far is one of the prime characteristics of immaturity. Children often plunge ahead recklessly, oblivious to anyone but themselves. They exercise no restraint or judgment. They are unaware of consequences, of how their own individual acts can have harmful or catastrophic effects on others and on society. And they have not yet formed any taste or values, which come only with maturity.

One *can* go too far.

If you go too far out on a cliff, you fall off; if you swim too far out in the ocean, you drown. Moderation and subtlety, as well as the awareness of the effects we each have on society, are part of maturity. These are basic values to be considered in every form of literature.

I'm all for breaking new ground in horror fiction. Experimentation is great. Being radical is fine. But there *are* limits. If you go "too far" in horror, you're not being a pioneer; you're being childish and self-indulgent. You are pandering to the perverted edge of society. You're contributing to the degradation of your audience because senseless horror, featuring gore for gore's sake, is desensitizing and dehumanizing.

Again, to quote Robert Bloch:

The chief danger . . . is not so much the violent content of today's fiction and film as it is the lack of any attitude of moral responsibility on the part of the creator . . . this business of saying, "Here it is, folks, a slice of life, raw and bleeding."

Splatterpunk versus Quiet Horror

Do I wish to stop such graphic horrors? Would I support an effort to censor such material? Absolutely not. I don't hold with censorship in any form. There's room in the genre for *all* types of work. The field of horror is broad enough to encompass "splatterpunk" as well as "quiet" horror, the experimental as well as the traditional, and I wouldn't want it any other way.

Skipp and Spector have every right to believe as they do, and to promote and participate in the splatterpunk movement. They have attracted, and will no doubt continue to attract, a certain portion of the horror audience—and graphic works dealing with raw, overt violence will probably always be with us. I do not believe, however, that the slice-and-dice school will ever dominate, or truly represent, the majority of readers and viewers.

It could be argued that I have included some very violent fiction in my anthology, *Urban Horrors*, thus negating my position. Not so. Several of the stories I chose deal with shocking horrors, but they do not *pander* to them. They neither promote nor encourage violence. They don't make violence sadistically attractive.

Writer-editor Charles L. Grant, who has always been a strong advocate of the less-is-more school, stated, "Violence has the same role in horror fiction as it has in any other kind of fiction. Where it is necessary, you use it, and where it's not, you don't. Gratuitous violence is vile."

On the other hand, Britain's Clive Barker, who gained overnight fame for his *Books of Blood*, claimed in "Faces of Darkness" (edited by Doug Winter):

> *You can never show too much. . . . Copious bloodletting works very well upon me. . . . My stories are not written primarily to terrify, but to excite. . . . Horror fiction without violence doesn't do a great deal for me. I think that death and wounding need to be in the air [and] there has to be something vile. I like to be able to deliver the vileness.*

One of Barker's favorite books is a medical text, a forensic casebook containing color photos of the victims of grotesque accidents and violent crimes. But even Barker has admitted, "I'm often disturbed by what I write. Sometimes I can even disgust myself with a notion."

This fascination with blood and excessive violence was discussed by

Katherine Ramsland (professor of philosophy at Rutgers University):

> [There are] sadomasochistic cults across the country. They find peace, strength, and satisfaction in drinking blood they extract in various ways — with needles, sometimes through a bite, sometimes through whippings and beatings. Their willing victims exchange blood for money or sexual favors. Others apparently find sexual release in masochistic submission.

The Power of Suggestion

I believe that a writer should not encourage or glorify this kind of real-life sickness with his or her fiction. In making overt violence and bloodletting attractive, such writers are, it seems to me, contributing to the breakdown of our society.

However, if handled with proper literary restraint and judgment, graphic horror *does* have its place in the genre, depending on the way it is presented.

A number of very talented writers, people I admire and respect, have dabbled successfully in graphic horror. I greatly enjoyed Joe Lansdale's violent novel, *The Nightrunners,* and I have already commented favorably on the strong writing in *The Silence of the Lambs,* by Thomas Harris. But it seems to me that these authors *do* know when to stop; they do not deliberately take their fiction "too far." Read them and judge for yourself. (Lansdale, by the way, dislikes being termed a splatterpunk.)

I have always felt that suggestion ultimately has more power than full revelation in the presentation of horror. Nothing is left to the imagination with totally explicit horror.

You will note that when I was constructing my tennis-court horror sequence (in Chapter Eight), I did *not* visually portray the Creature either murdering Ellen or ripping away one of her arms to use as a club. You *hear* her scream. Later, you experience the shock of encountering the arm-as-club at the climax of the sequence. Which is enough. I felt that there was nothing to be gained — that, in fact, there was much to lose — in an explicitly visual scene of her left arm being torn from her body.

For me, the most frightening scene in any horror film occurs in *The Haunting.* We are in the bedroom with the trembling characters when we hear a monstrous presence moving down the hall; we watch in shock as the bedroom door bulges and bends from the horrific force outside. We never *see* what causes this, but we experience its unsettling effect.

In classic horror, the imagination is stimulated; the author allows us to use our minds to fill in the gory details.

You might ask: Don't *genuinely* horrible things have to happen for the story to be taken seriously and for the threat to be real and frightening?

Yes, of course. What happens to the young boy and girl in Henry James's *The Turn of the Screw* is genuinely horrible, but the author uses subtle effects, dark hints, suggestions of terror and perversion; he is never explicit or obvious.

An Answer for Today's Horror

But the classics were all written many years ago, you protest. What about now, *today*, the 1990s? Should I write more boldly, graphically, along with the splatterpunk writers, or should I stick with the more traditional forms of horror?

I can't answer that for you. With my own fiction, I prefer to work the vast middle ground between the traditional and the excessive. You can be bold, experimental, modern — and still allow your readers to stretch their minds, to use their own imaginations. I don't avoid confrontations with violence in my work, but I never present it in attractive terms. I try, always, to respect my audience, to challenge them, to entertain them . . . not degrade them. I write to the *best*, not to the *beast*, in humankind.

In the final analysis, how *you* wish to write horror is entirely your own business. You must decide for yourself just how far you want to go with your work. This is your decision; no one else can make it for you.

In the beginning of this chapter, I told you that it was not easy to answer the question, "Just how graphic should horror be?" Each of us, as horror writers, must answer this question individually.

10.
A DIP IN "THE POOL"

T he best way for me to demonstrate the technique of writing an effective
horror story is to provide you with a step-by-step guide through one of
my own. In my analysis of "The Pool," you'll see how the plot is constructed, how the opening hook is utilized, how a sense of mounting suspense is achieved, how mood and texture contribute to the horror; you'll
see how dialogue is employed to move the plot forward and to reveal character, how the full description of the Creature is delayed, how and when
to switch point of view, and how sensory description is used to involve the
reader. I'll show you precisely how I shaped this story to deliver maximum
shock and fright.

The locale is Los Angeles, in the plush area of Bel Air, just beyond
Beverly Hills — and I begin with action, with my two main characters in a
moving car, making a turn off Sunset Boulevard:

> As they turned from Sunset Boulevard and drove past the high
> iron gates, swan-white and edged in ornamented gold, Lizbeth mut-
> tered under her breath.

In this opening sentence, with Lizbeth's reaction to the turn off Sunset, I
immediately set up tension. She's muttering. Something is wrong.

> "What's the matter with you?" Jaimie asked. "You just said 'shit,'
> didn't you?"
> "Yes, I said it."
> "Why?"
> She turned toward him in the MG's narrow bucket seat, frowning.
> "I said it because I'm angry. When I'm angry, I say 'shit.' "

"Which is my cue to ask why you're angry."

"I don't like jokes when it comes to something this important."

"So who's joking?"

"You are, by driving us here. You said *we were going to look at our new house."*

"We are. We're on the way."

"This is Bel Air, *Jaimie!"*

"Right. Says so, right on the gate."

"Obviously, the house isn't in Bel Air."

"Why obviously?"

"Because you made just $20,000 last year on commercials, and you haven't done a new one in three months. Part-time actors who earn $20,000 a year don't buy houses in Bel Air."

"Who says I bought it?"

She stared at him. *"You told me you* owned *it, that it was yours!"*

He grinned. *"It is, sweetcake. All mine."*

"I hate being called 'sweetcake.' It's a sexist term."

"Bullshit! It's a term of endearment."

"You've changed the subject."

"No, you did," *he said, wheeling the small sports roadster smoothly over the looping stretch of black asphalt.*

Lizbeth gestured toward the mansions flowing past along the narrow, climbing road, castles in sugar-cake pinks and milk-chocolate browns and pastel blues. *"So we're going to live in one of these?"* Her voice was edged in sarcasm.

Jaimie nodded, smiling at her. *"Just wait. You'll see!"*

Note that in this exchange between Jaimie and Lizbeth, I use dialogue to characterize them as sharply differing individuals. She's practical, pragmatic, a bit cynical, a romantic at heart. He's easy-going, smooth, a sporty type (drives an MG), willing to gamble with life. (All actors are gamblers.) We learn that he works in commercials but has no guaranteed salary, and that he made only $20,000 the previous year. (This is a very low income by Southern California entertainment-industry standards. The affluent residents of Bel Air normally earn *minimum* annual incomes in the high six figures.)

I also use their exchange to establish a mild conflict between them.

Jaimie is a bit of a male chauvinist, and Lizbeth resents this. And she thinks he's lying to her. Already, the reader can begin to relate to them as real people.

> *Under a cut-velvet driving cap, his tight-curled blond hair framed a deeply tanned, sensual actor's face. Looking at him, at that open, flashing smile, Lizbeth told herself once again that it was all too good to be true. Here she was, an ordinary small-town girl from Illinois, in her first year of theater arts at UCLA, about to hook up with a handsome young television actor who looked like Robert Redford and who now wanted her to live with him in Bel Air!*
>
> *Lizbeth had been in California for just over a month, had known Jaimie for only half that time, and was already into a major relationship. It was dreamlike. Everything had happened so fast: meeting Jaimie at the disco, his divorce coming through, getting to know his two kids, falling in love after just three dates.*
>
> *Life in California was like being caught inside one of those silent Chaplin films, where everything is speeded up and people whip dizzily back and forth across the screen. Did she* really *love Jaimie? Did he* really *love her? Did it matter?*
>
> *Just let it happen, kid, she told herself. Just flow with the action.*

To set up my narrative viewpoint, I have now entered the mind of Lizbeth, the true protagonist of the story, I have moved the story from the objective to the subjective. Through her thoughts and memories, we find out why she's here on this particular afternoon with Jaimie — and we learn about her background before they met. (By making her newly arrived in California, the speeded-up aspect of the locale can be explored through her fresh perspective; Jaimie takes it for granted.) We discover why Lizbeth came to California and what she's aiming for as a student. And again, through her, we learn much more about Jaimie: that he is now single, has two children, and is out to score a good time (demonstrated by where they met, in a disco).

We know that Lizbeth is physically attracted to his good looks and smile. (His smile will take on a special significance later in the story.) To Lizbeth, a small-town girl, Southern California offers a life in the fast lane. And she's willing to surrender to this swift, new lifestyle to live with a man she's known for just two weeks. Thus, her life has become dreamlike.

In this section, too, I have established the locale so that the reader is firmly rooted in the narrative.

"Here we are," said Jaimie, swinging the high-fendered little MG into a circular driveway of crushed white gravel. He braked the car, nodding toward the house. "Our humble abode!"

Lizbeth drew in a breath. Lovely! Perfect!

Not a mansion, which would have been too large and too intimidating, but a just-right two-story Spanish house topping a green-pine bluff, flanked by gardens and neatly trimmed box hedges.

"Well, do you like it?"

She giggled. "Silly question!"

"It's no castle."

"It's perfect! I hate big drafty places." She slid from the MG and stood looking at the house, hands on hips. "Wow. Oh, wow!"

"You're right about twenty-thou-a-year actors," he admitted, moving around the car to stand beside her. "This place is way beyond me."

"Then how did you . . . ?"

"I won it at poker last Thursday. High-stakes game. Went into it on borrowed cash. Got lucky, cleaned out the whole table, except for this tall, skinny guy who asks me if he can put up a house against what was in the pot. Said he had the deed on him and would sign it over to me if he lost the final hand."

"And you said yes."

"Damn right I did."

"And he lost?"

"Damn right he did."

She looked at the house and then back at him. "And it's legal?"

"The deed checks out. I own it all, Liz—house, gardens, pool."

"There's a pool?" Her eyes were shining.

He nodded. "And it's a beaut. Custom design. I may rent it out for commercials, pick up a little extra bread."

She hugged him. "Oh, Jaimie! I've always wanted to live in a house with a pool!"

"This one's unique."

"I want to see it!"

He grinned and then squeezed her waist. "First the house, then the pool. Okay?"

She gave him a mock bow. "Lead on, master!"

In this section, we have arrived at our central arena within the general locale: the house-grounds-pool area, where the real action of the story will be played. But take note: I did not allow Jaimie and Lizbeth to reach this specific area until I had established them fully as realistic characters with whom the reader could comfortably identify.

I now lessen the conflict between them as Jaimie explains to Lizbeth how he came to own the house, admitting that he could never afford it on his own. (I have planted a dramatic seed here, based on both the old saying "nothing in life is free" and the idea that there will be a price to pay for what he won in the game.)

Also—and this is important—I introduce the pool as a subject of conversation *before* I actually allow the reader to see it—thus giving it special dimension and meaning.

Lizbeth found it difficult to keep her mind on the house as Jaimie led her happily from room to room. Not that the place wasn't charming and comfortable, with its solid Spanish furniture, bright rugs, and beamed ceilings. But the prospect of finally having a pool of her own was so delicious that she couldn't stop thinking about it.

"I had a cleaning service come up here and get everything ready for us," Jaimie told her. He stood in the center of the living room, looking around proudly, reminding her of a captain on the deck of his first ship. "Place needed work. Nobody's lived here in ten years."

"How do you know that?"

"The skinny guy told me. Said he'd closed it down ten years ago, after his wife left him." He shrugged. "Can't say I blame her."

"What do you know about her?"

"Nothing. But the guy's a creep, a skinny creep." He flashed his white smile. "Women prefer attractive guys."

She wrinkled her nose at him. "Like you, right?"

"Right!"

He reached for her, but she dipped away from him, pulling off his cap and draping it over her dark hair.

"You look cute that way," he said.
"Come on, show me the pool. You promised to show me."
"Ah, yes, madame . . . the pool."

I have now introduced some disquieting elements. Although the house is very attractive, no one has lived in it for a full decade. The reader begins to wonder *why* the man shut down the place after his wife left. Also, the man is described as "a creep" (i.e., *creepy*). Again, I'm planting seeds in the reader's mind as I move toward my goal of setting up the specific arena of terror — the pool itself. Yet I still do not show the pool to the reader. By keeping Lizbeth away from it, I am teasing the reader, building tension as to what the pool is going to be like. By making Lizbeth anxious to see it, the *reader* becomes anxious — since she is the focal point for reader identification.

They had to descend a steep flight of weathered wooden steps to reach it. The pool was set in its own shelf of woodland terrain, notched into the hillside and screened from the house by a thick stand of trees.
"You never have to change the water," Jaimie said as they walked toward it. "Feeds itself from a stream inside the hill. It's self-renewing. Old water out, new water in. All the cleaning guys had to do was skim the leaves and stuff off the surface." He hesitated as the pool spread itself before them. "Bet you've never seen one like it!"
Lizbeth never had, not even in books or magazine photos.
It was huge, *at least ten times larger than she'd expected, edged on all sides by gray, angular rocks. It was designed in an odd, irregular shape that actually made her . . . made her . . . suddenly made her . . .*
Dizzy. I'm dizzy.
"What's wrong?"
"I don't know." She pressed a hand against her eyes. "I . . . I feel a little . . . sick."
"Are you having your . . . ?"
"No, it's not that. I felt fine until. . . ." She turned away toward the house. "I just don't like it."
"What don't you like?"
"The pool," she said, breathing deeply. "I don't like the pool. There's something wrong about it."

He looked confused. "I thought you'd love it!" His tone held irritation. "Didn't you just tell me you always wanted. . . ."

"Not one like this," she interrupted, overriding his words. "Not this one." She touched his shoulder. "Can we go back to the house now? It's cold here. I'm freezing."

He frowned. "But it's warm, Liz! Must be eighty at least. How can you be cold?"

She was shivering and hugging herself for warmth. "But I am! Can't you feel the chill?"

"All right," he sighed. "Let's go back."

She didn't speak during the climb up to the house.

Below them, wide and black and deep, the pool rippled its dark skin, a stirring, sluggish, patient movement in the windless afternoon.

With this section, I have introduced the pool itself in a very ominous way. Nothing seems normal about it; the pool is so strange ("an odd, irregular shape") that it makes Lizbeth dizzy. She *physically* senses the evil here, and suddenly has to get away. She is chilled, yet the weather is warm. (I am utilizing the legend that "cold spots" in a house indicate the presence of a ghost.) The fact that only Lizbeth feels the cold tells us that she alone is sensitive to the evil connected with the pool, and the reader strongly sympathizes with her.

Jaimie is set up as the patsy, the fellow who has no sensitivity to the dark things of the world.

And finally, with the last, one-line paragraph, I move the reader a step closer to terror by removing Lizbeth as a screen and allowing the reader to experience the evil directly. Is the pool itself alive? What powers does it possess? What's going to happen to Lizbeth (we *know* it's going to get Jaimie!)?

Upstairs, naked in the Spanish four-poster bed, Lizbeth could not imagine what had come over her at the pool. Perhaps the trip up to the house along the sharply winding road had made her carsick. Whatever the reason, by the time they were back in the house, the dizziness had vanished, and she'd enjoyed the curried chicken dinner Jaimie had cooked for them. They'd sipped white wine by a comforting hearth fire and then made love there tenderly late into the night, with the pulsing flame tinting their bodies in shades of pale gold.

"Jan and David are coming by in the morning," he had told her. "Hope you don't mind."

"Why should I? I think your kids are great."

"I thought we'd have this first Sunday together, just the two of us; but school starts for them next week, and I promised they could spend the day here."

"I don't mind. Really I don't."

He kissed the tip of her nose. "That's my girl."

"The skinny man. . . ."

"What about him?"

"I don't understand why he didn't try to sell this house in the ten years when he wasn't living here."

"I don't know. Maybe he didn't need the money."

"Then why bet it on a poker game? Surely the pot wasn't anywhere near equal to the worth of this place."

"It was just a way for him to stay in the game. He had a straight flush and thought he'd win."

"Was he upset at losing the place?"

Jaimie frowned at that question. "Now that you mention it, he didn't seem to be. He took it very calmly."

"You said that he left after his wife split. Did he talk about her at all?"

"He told me her name."

"Which was?"

"Gail. Her name was Gail."

Having established the aura of evil, I now set up a quiet, romantic interlude, a deliberate change of pace to show how close Lizbeth becomes to Jaimie (making his loss, later in the story, more emotionally painful). Also, I plant the fact that his children will be coming to the house (which will be paid off dramatically at the story's end).

The dialogue is important here: it tells us that the skinny man had no intention of selling the house and only put it up for wager when he thought he had a winning hand. But when he *did* lose it, he made no complaint; what happens to Jaimie is up to fate. He need feel no guilt; the skinny man did not *intend* for Jaimie to die at the house.

And finally, for the first time, we learn the name of the man's wife.

Now, lying in the upstairs bed, Lizbeth wondered what had hap-
pened to Gail. It was odd somehow to think that she and the skinny
man had made love in this same bed. In a way, she'd taken Gail's place.

Lizbeth still felt guilty about saying no to Jaimie when he'd sug-
gested a postmidnight swim. "Not tonight, darling. I've a slight head-
ache. Too much wine, maybe. You go on without me."

And so he'd gone on down to the pool alone, telling her that such
a mild, late-summer night was just too good to waste, that he'd take a
few laps around the pool and be back before she finished her cigarette.

Irritated with herself, Lizbeth stubbed out the glowing Pall Mall in
the bedside ashtray. Smoking was a filthy habit — ruins your lungs,
stains your teeth. And smoking in bed was doubly stupid. You fall asleep
. . . the cigarette catches the bed on fire. She must stop smoking. All it
took was some real will power, and if . . .

Lizbeth sat up abruptly, easing her breath to listen. Nothing. No
sound.

That was wrong. The open bedroom window overlooked the pool,
and she'd been listening, behind her thoughts, to Jaimie splashing
about below in the water.

Now she suddenly realized that the pool sounds had ceased, to-
tally.

She smiled at her own nervous reaction. The silence simply
meant that Jaimie had finished his swim and was out of the pool and
headed back to the house. He'd be there any second.

But he didn't arrive.

This is a transitional section, in which I ease the reader toward oncoming
terrors. I have now separated the lovers, isolating my protagonist in the
house and situating Jaimie at the pool. I show Lizbeth's apprehensive state
of mind, and I use *silence* as an element of suspense. Where is Jaimie, and
why hasn't he returned to the bedroom? We *know* that something terrible
has happened to him at the pool. But what? Thus, I build my suspense,
layer by layer, tightening the story's grip on the reader.

Lizbeth moved to the window. Moonlight spilled across her breasts
as she leaned forward to peer out into the night. The pale mirror glim-
mer of the pool flickered in the darkness below, but the bulk of trees
screened it from her vision.

"Jaimie!" Her voice pierced the silence. "Jaimie, are you still down there!"

No reply. Nothing from the pool. She called his name again, without response.

Had something happened while he was swimming? Maybe a sudden stomach cramp or a muscle spasm from the cold water? No, he would have called out for help. She would have heard him.

Then . . . what? Surely this was no practical joke, an attempt to scare her? No, impossible. That would be cruel, and Jaimie's humor was never cruel. But he might think of it as fun, a kind of hide-and-seek in a new house. Damn him!

Angry now, she put on a nightrobe and stepped into her slippers. She hurried downstairs, out the back door, across the damp lawn, to the pool steps.

"Jaimie! If this is a game, I don't like it! Damn it, I mean that!" *She peered downward; the moonlit steps were empty.* "Answer *me!"*

Then, muttering "Shit!" under her breath, she started down the clammy wooden steps, holding to the cold iron pipe rail. The descent seemed even more precipitous in the dark, and she forced herself to move slowly.

Reaching level ground, Lizbeth could see the pool. She moved closer for a full view. It was silent and deserted. Where was Jaimie? She suddenly was gripped by the familiar sense of dizzy nausea as she stared at the odd, weirdly angled rock shapes forming the pool's perimeter. She tried to look away. And couldn't.

It wants me!

That terrible thought seized her mind. But what wanted her? The pool? No . . . something in the pool.

This sequence is the kickoff to the horror that Lizbeth is about to encounter, and the reader is warning her, *don't* go down there, *don't* go to that pool! (Echoes of *Don't open that door!*)

Note the way I have structured this scene and the elements I have used in it. First, Lizbeth is *alone,* and her nakedness makes her vulnerable (as Janet Leigh was vulnerable in *Psycho*). Putting on the robe does little to lessen her sense of basic vulnerability. The trees screen the pool from her, adding frustration. I use anger as the thing that propels her out of the house, into the hostile dark; she's mad at Jaimie for causing all this.

But at the point I have Lizbeth moving down the steps toward the pool, I switch her mood from anger to wariness, as the descent proves more difficult. Then, as she walks toward the pool, the dizzy nausea returns — and I use the odd *shape* of the pool to help induce it.

Now she's in the orbit of whatever evil is there, in the hypnotic grip of the pool, and it's too late for a retreat. The reader knows Lizbeth can't go back, and with her thought *"it wants me,"* the point of ultimate terror has been reached.

The final line reveals, for the first time, that it is not the pool itself that is evil, it's what is *in* the pool. Another layer of suspense has been uncovered — and just as Lizbeth can't look away from the pool, the reader cannot look away from the page.

Note my use of the five senses in this scene: *sound* (as her voice breaks the silence), *touch* ("holding to the cold iron pipe rail"), *sight* (as she sees the pool), *taste* (the nausea), even *smell* in an understated way (one can imagine the odor rising from "the clammy wooden steps"). Thus, I am totally involving the reader in a tactile, fully dimensional environment of dread.

> *She kicked off the bedroom slippers and found herself walking toward the pool across moon-sparkled grass, spiky and cold against the soles of her bare feet.*
>
> Stay back! Stay away from it!
>
> *But she couldn't. Something was drawing her toward the black pool, something she could not resist.*
>
> *At the rocks, facing the water, she unfastened her nightrobe, allowing it to slip free of her body.*
>
> *She was alabaster under the moon, a subtle curving of leg, of thigh, of neck and breast. Despite the jarring fear hammer of her heart, Lizbeth knew that she had to step forward into the water.*
>
> It wants me!
>
> *The pool was black glass, and she looked down into it, at the reflection of her body, like white fire on the still surface.*
>
> *Now . . . a ripple, a stirring, a deep-night movement from below.*
>
> *Something was coming — a shape, a dark mass, gliding upward toward the surface.*
>
> *Lizbeth watched, hypnotized, unable to look away, unable to obey*

the screaming, pleading voice inside her: Run! Run!

And then she saw Jaimie's hand. It broke the surface of the pool, reaching out to her.

His face bubbled free of the clinging black water, and acid bile leaped into her throat. She gagged, gasped for air, her eyes wide in sick shock.

It was part *Jaimie, part something else!*

It smiled at her with Jaimie's wide, white-toothed open mouth, but, oh God! only one of its eyes belonged to Jaimie. It had three others, all horribly different. It had part *of Jaimie's face, part of his body.*

Run! Don't go to it! Get away!

But Lizbeth did not run. Gently, she folded her warm, pinkfleshed hand into the icy wet horror of that hand in the pool and allowed herself to be drawn slowly forward. Downward. As the cold, receiving waters shocked her skin, numbing her, as the black liquid rushed into her open mouth, into her lungs and stomach and body, filling her as a cup is filled, her final image, the last thing she saw before closing her eyes, was Jaimie's wide-lipped, shining smile — an expanding patch of brightness fading down . . . deep . . . very deep . . . into the pool's black depths.

In this section, the horror is fully realized. Lizbeth, under the spell of the thing in the pool, is taken into its depths, drawn there by the hand of her lover. The last image I give the reader is that of Jaimie's smile, a subtle reversal of the norm (death is no smiling matter).

This entire section is deliberately sensual; she is responding, naked and open, to the call of her lover. She gags, is horrified, but finally gives in to the pool-thing. Note that once the water closes over her I do *not* break the sentence; I allow the words and images to carry the reader down with her, all the way to the bottom of the pool.

Jan and David arrived early that Sunday morning, all giggles and shouts, breathing hard from the ride on their bikes.

A whole Sunday with Dad. A fine, warm-sky summer day with school safely off somewhere ahead and not bothering them. A big house to roam in, and yards to run in, and caramel-ripple ice cream waiting (Dad had promised to buy some!), and games to play, and . . .

"Hey! Look what I found!"

Jan was yelling at David. They had gone around to the back of the house when no one answered the bell, looking for their father. Now eight-year-old Jan was at the bottom of a flight of high wooden steps, yelling up at her brother. David was almost ten and tall for his age.

"What you find?"

"Come and see!"

He scrambled down the steps to join her.

"Jeez!" he said. "A pool! I never saw one this big before!"

"Me neither."

David looked over his shoulder, up at the silent house.

"Dad's probably out somewhere with his new girlfriend."

"Probably," Jan agreed.

"Let's try the pool while we're waiting. What do you say?"

"Yeah, let's!"

They began pulling off their shirts.

My story *could* have ended with Lizbeth's death, but I often enjoy providing what I term a *double climax*, giving the reader another unexpected jolt. When the two kids show up, I change the mood and point of view completely: they arrive in bright sunlight, full of happiness and energy. Then they find the pool, and the reader is shocked to realize they're going to *swim* there. And, like their father, they sense nothing amiss; they are totally unaware of the thing that waits for them.

Motionless in the depths of the pool, at the far end, where rock and tree shadows darkened the surface, it waited, hearing the tinkling high child voices filtering down to it in the sound-muted waters. It was excited because it had never absorbed a child; a child was new and fresh — new pleasures, new strengths.

It had formed itself within the moist deep soil of the hill, and the pool had nurtured and fed it, helping it grow, first with small, squirming water bugs and other yard insects. It had absorbed them, using their eyes and their hard, metallic bodies to shape itself. Then the pool had provided a dead bird, and now it had feathers along part of its back, and the bird's sharp beak formed part of its face. Then a plump gray rat had been drawn into the water, and the rat's glassy eye became part of the thing's body. A cat had drowned here, and its claws and matted fur added new elements to the thing's expanding mass.

Finally, when it was still young, a golden-haired woman, Gail, had come here alone to swim that long-ago night, and the pool had taken her, given her as a fine new gift to the thing in its depths. And Gail's long silk-gold hair streamed out of the thing's mouth (one of its mouths, for it had several), and it had continued to grow, to shape itself.

Then, last night, this man, Jaimie, had come to it. And his right eye now burned like blue phosphor from the thing's face. Lizbeth had followed, and her slim-fingered hands, with their long, lacquered nails, now pulsed in wormlike convulsive motion along the lower body of the pool-thing.

Now it was excited again, trembling, ready for new bulk, new lifestuffs to shape and use. It rippled in dark anticipation, gathering itself, feeling the pleasure and the hunger.

Faintly, above it, the boy's cry: "Last one in's a fuzzy green monkey!"

It rippled to the vibrational splash of two young bodies striking the water.

It glided forward swiftly toward the children.

Thus, I end the story from the viewpoint of the horror within the pool. Only at this very late point do I allow the reader to know just what is down there, how it was formed, and what it actually looks like. Many beginning writers make the mistake of telling too much too soon, of describing the horror in detail at the start of their story. I create an element of mystery with the thing in the pool; I withhold its shape and function until the final page.

I always take great care with the closing line of a horror story. Ideally, the line should leave the reader with yet more terrors to be realized beyond the end of the narrative itself — my *echo effect*. (See my comments on the echo effect in Chapter Eight.)

It's Your Turn

What I have done with "The Pool," in the way of detailed analysis, *you* can do with stories of your own choosing. Select a horror story that you liked the first time you read it. Carefully reread it. Get the overall story fixed in your mind. Then go back and read it section by section, breaking it down as to basic structure, plot elements, characterization, and conflict. Dissect it; find out *why* the story is successful, *why* it is frightening, and exactly *how* the author achieved suspense and terror. Note how narrative viewpoint and dialogue illuminate situations and locales, how actions are related to character, and how the author builds to the climax.

This kind of analysis will help you understand the *mechanics* of horror fiction. (You can do the same thing, on a larger scale, with favorite novels.) The process is similar to taking apart the engine of a car to see how the parts all work together to produce the power. Once you understand how it's been done by other writers, you can successfully build your own fictional engines.

Analysis pays.

11.
WHEN THE CRYPT IS SEALED

What Goes into the construction of an effective ending for a horror story or novel?

First and foremost, your ending must *satisfy* the reader. It must be a logical extension of the narrative, the inevitable result of events that you set in motion earlier. Readers must be emotionally prepared for your ending. It cannot feel forced; rather, it must grow from the soil of your narrative, from your characters, and from their problems and conflict.

Clarity is vital; your ending should not be ambiguous; it should not leave readers muttering, "What happened?"

Which is not to say that you can't surprise the reader once the clues that make the surprise logical have been previously planted. If the rules of logic have not been violated, readers love to be surprised. Your ending can be as fantastic as you wish to make it so long as it's consistent with the *type* of fantasy you have set up in the story. (No werewolves turning into vampires in the last chapter; no ghosts becoming demons.)

In "One of Those Days," for example, I draw the portrait of a man who has mentally broken down. He heads for his psychiatrist, Dr. Mellowthin, in the hope that the doctor can help. But this man is beyond help. At Mellowthin's office, he begins to recount details of his mental breakdown when he suddenly sits up on the couch:

> *I opened my eyes and stared at Dr. Mellowthin.*
> *"What's the matter?" he asked, somewhat uneasily.*
> *"Well," I said, "to begin with, you have large brown, sad-looking, liquidy eyes."*
> *"And . . ."*

"And I bet your nose is cold!" I grinned.

"Anything else?"

"Not really."

"What about my overall *appearance?"*

"Well, of course, you're covered with long black shaggy hair, even down to the tips of your big floppy ears."

A moment of strained silence.

"Can you do tricks?" I asked.

"A few," Mellowthin replied, shifting in his chair.

"Roll over!" I commanded.

He did.

"Play dead!"

His liquidy eyes rolled up white and his long pink tongue lolled loosely from his jaws.

"Good doggie," I said. "Nice doggie."

"Woof," barked Dr. Mellowthin softly, wagging his tail.

I tossed him a bone I'd saved from the garden and left his office.

There was no getting around it.

This was simply one of those days.

Although the story is handled with a lightness of style, the humor is dark indeed. The surprise at the end is that Dr. Mellowthin has turned into a shaggy dog. But the reader knows this transformation is real *only* in the mind of the protagonist. Thus, when he leaves the office, we know he has taken the final step into madness.

The reader accepts my ending because I have laid the proper groundwork for it.

End of Conflict = End of Tale

Another primary rule: Avoid anticlimax. Don't ramble on beyond your final, climactic scene. Your story ends when the conflict has been resolved. The suspense is over and it's time to bring down the curtain.

If a monster (any type of menace) is involved, the protagonist should ideally prevail against the monster in a final showdown. When the menace has been defeated, the book ends.

Consider how Stephen King winds up the last chapter of *The Dark Half*:

Be careful, Thaddeus. No man controls the agents of the after life. Not for long—and there is always a price.

What price will I have to pay? *he wondered coldly. then:* And the bill—when does it come due?

But . . . perhaps the bill had been paid.

Perhaps he was finally even.

"Is he dead?" Liz was asking, almost begging.

"Yes," Thad said. "He's dead, Liz. . . . The book is closed on George Stark. Come on, you guys, let's get out of here."

And that was what they did.

The hero's monstrous dark half, George Stark, has been vanquished. Good has triumphed over evil.

But does the monster *always* have to die?

Of course not. There have been countless novels and stories published in which the monster triumphs. But the same rules of logic must prevail.

In Shirley Jackson's classic short story, "The Lottery," the people of a small village perform a traditional act, in which a neighbor is stoned to death. Individually, they are not monsters, but as a mob, they become a killing force. Jackson's dark ending is totally logical, given the local traditions of the village:

> *The children had stones already, and someone gave little Davy Hutchison a few pebbles.*
>
> *Tessie Hutchison was in the center of a cleared space by now, and she held her hands out desperately as the villagers moved in on her.*
>
> *"It isn't fair," she said. A stone hit her on the side of the head.*
>
> *Old Man Warner was saying, "Come on, come on, everyone."* . . .
>
> *"It isn't fair, it isn't right," Mrs. Hutchison screamed, and then they were upon her.*

In my story "Dead Call," the narrator *becomes* the monster after being talked into suicide by a dead friend. Now, the narrator is poised to talk others into acts of self-destruction. I end my story by having the narrator directly address the reader:

I've been dead for a month now, and Len was right. It's fine here. No pressures. No worries. Gray and quiet and beautiful . . .

I know how lousy things have been for you. And they're not going to improve.

Isn't that your phone ringing?

Better answer it.

It's important that we talk.

Many dark endings are circular—returning to their beginnings. In "The Partnership," I begin the story in Sally's cafe, as my protagonist, Tad Miller, observes a fancy watch on the wrist of a stranger. Tad engages him in talk, takes the stranger to an abandoned amusement park, feeds him to his "partner," Ed, then takes the fancy watch. In my end scene, he uses this watch as the lure for another stranger—and Tad's final question brings the story full circle:

> *Three and a half weeks later the stranger at the counter in Sally's was looking at my watch.*
>
> *"I've never seen one like that," he said.*
>
> *"Tells you the time in ten parts of the world," I said. "Tells you the month of the year and the day of the week. And it rings every hour on the hour."*
>
> *The stranger was impressed.*
>
> *After a while, I grinned, leaned toward him across the counter and said, "You ever go to amusement parks as a kid?"*

In other endings, the evil is not *quite* vanquished. The author is telling his readers that although the monster was overcome *this* time, it may have latent powers; the ultimate threat may still exist.

As in *Usher's Passing* by Robert R. McCammon:

> *Was it over? he wondered. Would it ever really be over? Or would the evil just take some other form and come back strong—maybe looking for him?*
>
> *If so, he had to be ready.*

Then again, some endings *seem* to tell us the monster is dead, but a lingering doubt is expressed.

As in Thomas Tessier's *The Nightwalker*:

> *[She] . . . stood by her bedroom window in the gray light of early morning. She stared, unseeing, at the tiny garden outside and the worn brick buildings immediately beyond. Only fire and silver could end it, but they didn't know that. Yet, somehow, . . . she had come to be sure that Bobby Ives was finally still. To work was out of the question; she must cancel her appointments for the day. Perhaps she would take a walk. A good long walk.*

The Tone of the Ending

If the monster wins, can the ending still be upbeat? Yes and no. In *Rosemary's Baby*, by Ira Levin, the devil cult is victorious — and Rosemary gives birth to a satanic baby with glowing red eyes. She's been fighting the cult all through the novel, but once she actually *sees* her newborn baby, the maternal instinct takes over; the book ends "happily" with Rosemary's acceptance of her devil-child:

> *Rosemary tickled the baby's tummy. . . . She poked the tip of his nose. "Do you know how to smile yet, Andy? Do you? Come on, little funny-eyes Andy, can you . . . smile for Mommy?" . . .*
> *The Japanese slipped forward with his camera, crouched, and took two three four pictures in quick succession.*

In Ramsey Campbell's "The Chimney," a boy survives a terror-filled childhood but ends up with severe self-doubts as to life's "happy" outcome:

> *My mother came to live with us, but we could see she was pining; my parents must have loved each other, in their way. She died a year later. Perhaps I killed them both. I know that what emerged from the chimney was in some sense my father. But surely that was a premonition. Surely my fear could never have reached out to make him die that way.*

Then there are endings wherein the horrors the characters have endured have crippled their lives — as in Joe Lansdale's *The Nightrunners*:

Becky . . . wondered how it would be now for Monty and her. She felt oddly certain there would be no more images and black dreams living in her head. But how would they see the world now? They had been over on the darkside and tasted a moment without rules and logic; and once those rules had been broken, shattered like wine crystal, she wondered if those pieces could ever be gathered and properly glued again.

She could only hope, and the ability to do that, to hope, meant everything to her.

Irony is often present in the endings of horror stories. The conflict is over, but the results have meaning beyond what is realized by the character. In my sniper story, "A Real Nice Guy," I present a sexual encounter between two strangers. Jimmie (whom the reader knows to be a vicious, police-hunted sniper) goes to bed with Janet. At the end, she shoots him from a rooftop as he comes out of an apartment building. Turns out they were *both* snipers (though neither of them knew the truth about the other). Thus, irony is achieved in my closing paragraphs:

Poor Jimmie, she thought. It was just his bad luck to meet me. *But that's the way it goes.*

Janet Lakely had a rule, and she never broke it; when you bed down a guy in a new town you always target him the next day. She sighed. Usually it didn't bother her. Most of them were bastards. But not Jimmie. She'd enjoyed talking to him, playing her word games with him . . . bedding him. She was sorry he had to go.

He seemed like a real nice guy.

In horror, you can get away with negative, unhappy endings in short stories much easier than you can in novels. This is because, in a much longer narrative, the readers have sweated out the adventure and trials with your protagonist, and they wish to share the final victory. They feel cheated otherwise. They have more *invested* in a novel, and it's a letdown to them if things turn out badly.

In a short story, you can end on a note of coming disaster, bitter irony, or outright defeat—and get away with it. Your readers will not object to this type of windup since you have not put them through 300 pages of tension and terror to reach the climax.

Many times, a happy ending leaves the characters with a job to be done before their *ultimate* happiness can be realized. Dean Koontz's *Midnight* offers an example:

> *Scott had stopped struggling. He was probably just exhausted. Sam was sure that he had not really gotten through the boy's rage. Hadn't more than scratched the surface. Sam had let an evil into their lives, the evil of self-indulgent despair, which he transmitted to the boy, and now rooting it out would be a hard job. They had a long way to go, months of struggle, maybe even years, lots of hugging, lots of holding on tight and not letting go.*
>
> *Looking over Scott's shoulder, he saw that Tessa and Chrissie had stepped into the room. They were crying too. In their eyes he saw an awareness that matched his, a recognition that the battle for Scott had only begun.*
>
> *But it* had *begun. That was the wonderful thing. It* had *begun.*

Other happy endings involve a change of locale for the surviving characters. They want to get away, escape, find a fresh environment to begin their lives anew.

Peter Straub demonstrates this approach on the final page of *If You Could See Me Now*:

> *She straightened her back on the seat beside me. There [was] no more crying . . . "Let's just drive," she said. "I don't want to see Zack. . . . We can write from wherever we get to."*
>
> *"Fine," I said.*
>
> *"Let's go someplace like Wyoming or Colorado."*
>
> *"Whatever you want," I said.*

Avoid a Circumstantial Monster

Another primary rule in horror: Don't cheat your readers. You should rigorously avoid explaining away the horror at the end, telling the readers there never was a *real* threat at all, that the menace just *seemed* to be real, that it was all based on circumstantial evidence or on a series of deliberate misconceptions. Do this and you anger your readers. They invested their time and emotions for nothing; they trusted you while you made fools of them. If you promise a werewolf, you'd better damn well deliver one, not a man in a fright mask.

Even as a child, long before I became a writer, I hated this type of dramatic deception. The old radio program "Inner Sanctum" was constantly guilty of this. At the end of each show, all of the seemingly supernatural events were revealed as phony, staged to trap one of the characters, or to frighten the villain, or whatever. I was always furious at having been duped, and once I realized what the show was up to, I quit listening.

It's Not Over Till It's Over: The Shocking Final Line

Many writers have utilized the *shocking final line* technique in ending their stories and novels. This works particularly well in horror stories — as demonstrated in Ray Bradbury's graveyard chiller, "The Emissary":

> Dog was a bad dog, digging where he shouldn't. Dog was a good dog, always making friends. Dog loved people. Dog brought them home.
>
> And now, moving up the dark hall stairs, at intervals, came the sound of feet, one foot dragged after the other, painfully, slowly, slowly, slowly.
>
> Dog shivered. A rain of strange night earth fell seething on the bed.
>
> Dog turned.
>
> The bedroom door whispered in.
>
> Martin had company.

The last line in Lord Dunsany's tale "Two Bottles of Relish" is classic. In the story, a man has killed his wife and has cooked and eaten her body. At the end, the police inspector is curious about *why* the killer exerted himself by chopping down a number of trees.

> They walked through our sitting room in silence . . . and together they went into the hall, and there I heard the only words they said to each other. It was the inspector that first broke that silence.
>
> "But why," he said, "did he cut down the trees?"
>
> "Solely," said Linley, "in order to get an appetite."

I have included a cross-sampling of endings, happy and unhappy, shocking and ironic, to illustrate the wide variety possible within the genre. Each is valid and appropriate. Each has been properly and carefully set up by the author.

Therefore, always keep in mind the central rule I have demonstrated throughout this chapter: Whatever your ending, it must *fit*.

12.
FINDING A HOME FOR YOUR HORROR

A ll right, now that you know about writing horror, just where do you *sell* it?

Many writers begin their careers with short fiction, gradually working toward novels as their skills increase and they gain confidence in their ability to handle plot and characterization. A novel requires, at the very least, several months to write, and if it is rejected by publishers, the blow to your ego may be severe enough to discourage further effort. A short story can be completed in a single evening (I've written them in an hour), and if the story fails to gain acceptance with an editor, no great emotional harm is done in terms of rejection. You just go ahead and write another.

Small-Press Magazines

Therefore, let's begin with the best market for short stories: the small-press magazines.

For the beginner, without credits in the genre, I would strongly urge submission to this market. If your story demonstrates real talent, even if that talent has not yet been refined and polished, you still have a very good chance to see your work reach print in a small-press magazine. The editors are always open to new writers, and your track record in the genre is of no consequence.

The catch is, they can't afford to pay you. These magazines operate on a nonprofit basis; costs of production, printing, distribution, and postage are paid by the publisher-editor. The illustrations in each issue are donated by beginning artists attempting to perfect their craft as you are attempting, as writers, to perfect yours. There just isn't any money to pay contributors;

the entire project is a true labor of love. The people behind these modest little publications are willing to invest their time, money, and hard work to add something worthwhile to the genre they love. In doing so, they provide a platform for new writers and artists from which major careers may be launched. You'd be amazed to discover how many name writers in the field began by having their early fiction printed in such magazines. (I began my career that way and have continued to support these small magazines down through the years by donating work to them.)

This is a very flexible market—which is another way of saying it isn't very stable. The editors of such publications are usually attempting to break into the paying professional markets themselves, and they will often terminate their magazines once they've made a breakthrough.

For example, two of the best small-press magazines were recently shut down for this reason, as Paul Olson of *Horrorstruck* and David Silva of *The Horror Show* became active professionals. (Their two magazines had become so successful that the publisher-editors were actually able to pay their contributors. Not a lot, but you *did* get paid.)

Thus, the magazines listed below may or may not still be in operation by the time you submit to them. But if any of them *have* closed down, others will have sprung up to fill the ranks. For beginning writers, the market is always there.

Dead of Night
P.O. Box 682, East Long, MA 01028
Noctulpa
P.O. Box 5175, Long Island City, NY 11105
2 A.M.
P.O. Box 6754, Rockford, IL 61125-1754
Grue
P.O. Box 370, Times Square Station, New York, NY 10108
Eldritch Tales
1051 Wellington Road, Lawrence, KS 66044
Cemetery Dance
P.O. Box 858, Edgewood, MD 21040
New Blood
540 W. Foothill Boulevard, #3730, Glendora, CA 91740

After Hours
21541 Oakbrook, Mission Viejo, CA 92692
FantasyMacabre
P.O. Box 20610, Seattle, WA 98102
Haunts
P.O. Box 3342, Providence, RI 02906-0742
Deathrealm
3223-F, Regents Park, Greensboro, NC 27405
Starsong
Rt. 2, Box 260-B, St. Matthews, SC 29135
MidnightGraffiti
13101 Sudan Rd., Poway, CA 92064
The Sterling Web
P.O. Box 38383, Tallahassee, FL 32315
The Scream Factory
145 Tully Road, San Jose, CA 95111

Professional Magazines

Moving up to the professional magazine level, you'll find the market some-what thin at the moment. The recent demise of *Night Cry* and *Twilight Zone Magazine* has left just two publications. The first of these, *The Magazine of Fantasy and Science Fiction*, is a monthly that publishes some dark fantasy. The second, *Weird Tales*, is a quarterly (carrying on the tradition of the original pulp) and carries a larger proportion of horror fiction than does the former.

Two more genre magazines are on the horizon. Charles L. Grant has promised to launch a new, dark-fantasy magazine, *Shadows*, named after his recently retired series of anthologies. However, I have no address or further details.

Checking *Novel and Short Story Writer's Market* will give you more in-formation about all the publications just discussed—the current editor, rates, and so on.

Also, *Iniquities*, a new, slick-paper, horror magazine originating in Los Angeles, is due for publication in 1990 (167 North Sierra Bonita Avenue, Pasadena, California 91106).

These publications may or may not become active markets for horror.

In Great Britain, the two primary magazines are *Fear* (Box 10, Ludlow, Shrops, SY8 1DB, United Kingdom), and *Fantasy Tales* (194 Station Road, King's Heath, Birmingham, B14, 7TE, United Kingdom).

But what if you live in an ice cave in Twoshoes, Alaska, and can't hop down to the corner newsstand to check out the latest publications? One of the best ways to keep up with the publishing industry (and the film and TV world) is to subscribe to *Locus*, the monthly news-and-review magazine for the SF/fantasy/horror field. Charles Brown, its publisher-editor, has won many awards for this invaluable publication, and it is well worth your time and money. Write to:

Locus Publications
P.O. Box 13305
Oakland, CA 94661

Book Publishers

Beyond magazines, we move into the book markets. For shorter fiction, we have the publication each year of several "original" genre anthologies, featuring all new material. Unhappily for the beginner, most of the slots in such volumes are filled by invitation only. The editor contacts a number of well-known horror writers and asks them to submit new stories. Thus, the books are usually closed to the outsider. When there are editors who are willing to accept new writers in their anthologies, *Locus* will have the names and addresses.

The market for novels, however, is still open and quite active. Book publishers are constantly seeking new novelists, and if your talent is strong and original and you're willing to gamble your time and energy on a novel of at least 75,000 words, then there are several publishers receptive to your work.

I'm going to provide you with a current group of publishers who regularly issue books in the horror genre. Chances are, if the work is really good, one of them will accept your manuscript. They're certainly worth a shot.

Avon Books
105 Madison Avenue
New York, NY 10016

Bantam Books
666 Fifth Avenue
New York, NY 10103

Berkley Publishing Group
(including Charter and Jove)
200 Madison Avenue
New York, NY 10016

Dark Harvest (a specialty-press publisher)
P.O. Box 941
Arlington Heights, IL 60006

DAW Books
1633 Broadway
New York, NY 10019

Del Rey Books
201 East 50th Street
New York, NY 10022

Dell Books
(Dell Publishing Co.)
245 East 47th Street
New York, NY 10017

Doubleday and Co.
245 Park Avenue
New York, NY 10167

Leisure Books
(Dorchester Publishing Co.)
6 East 39th Street
New York, NY 10016

Pinnacle Books
475 Park Avenue South
New York, NY 10016

Pocket Books
1230 Avenue of the Americas
New York, NY 10020

St. Martin's Press
175 Fifth Avenue
New York, NY 10010

Scream/Press (a specialty-press publisher)
P.O. Box 481146
Los Angeles, CA 90048

Signet Books
(New American Library)
1633 Broadway
New York, NY 10019

Tor Books
49 West 24th Street
New York, NY 10010

Underwood-Miller (a specialty-press publisher)
708 Westover Drive
Lancaster, PA 17601

Warner Books
666 Fifth Avenue
New York, NY 10103

Zebra Books
475 Park Avenue South
New York, NY 10016

Mark V. Ziesing Books (a specialty-press publisher)
P.O. Box 76
Shingletown, CA 96088

The Entertainment Industry: Films and Television

I want to add a few thoughts relating to films and television. The entertainment industry is pretty much a closed market in terms of outside submissions from new writers. If you publish a book that has strong dramatic potential, you may be able to option your novel to a producer as a feature film, or to a network as a TV Movie of the Week. That's how I got started in the industry.

By the time I wrote my first novel, *Logan's Run*, I had been a published professional for eleven years. The book was purchased and produced as a major film by MGM starring Michael York, then was developed as a CBS television series starring Gregory Harrison.

Logan's Run was sold through an agent. Agents are *not* a necessity for beginning prose writers. Usually, you must place enough material in books and magazines to prove solid talent before a literary agent will take you on as a client. As a prose writer, if you want an agent, you must earn one.

However, for films and television, agents are your bridge to the producers. You *must* have a film/TV agent to function professionally in the entertainment industry.

Here's how it's done by many writers:

Let's say you're more than a beginning prose writer. You've had a number of your short stories printed in small-press publications, and you've even sold a few stories to the professional markets. From one of your writer friends, you hear about an agent who's looking for new clients. You submit a good sampling of your published work, and the agent agrees to represent you.

Through your literary agent, you are able to sell a novel, which is then published. It is prime movie material: visually written, with a strong plot and interesting, well-drawn characters. Your agent may decide to submit your book to various West Coast entertainment-industry agents who might be willing to "shop it around" to producers, studios, networks, and cable television. Meanwhile, every production-development executive in Hollywood is desperately searching for that perfect project that could become the next major box-office or TV success. Chances are, if your book has any possibility of big- or small-screen success, it will be read in galleys or in published form by a number of different development people from different companies. Competition is fierce in Hollywood, and *everybody* wants to grab the next up-and-coming ratings buster.

If you can get one of these companies to option your book, then you have a toehold in the industry. With active option negotiations on the agenda, you're certain to attract an entertainment-industry agent. On an informal and unofficial basis, one of the production executives may recommend you to an agent he or she knows. As an alternative, the Writers Guild of America, west* publishes a list that includes WGAw-approved agents and that can be purchased by anyone. (*The Writers Guild of

America, west, is located at 8955 Beverly Boulevard, Los Angeles, CA 90048-2456; Telephone (213)550-1000.) This list indicates which agencies will consider representing outside writers. It is to your advantage to be represented *only* by a WGAw-approved agent. Such agents have signed an agreement that protects the rights of WGAw members. Even though you, as a beginning entertainment-industry writer, do not yet belong to the Guild, you will still be more protected than if you dealt with a non-WGAw-approved agent.

But right now, if you're just getting started as a writer, don't worry about an agent. Just get those stories and novels written and in the mail. The old saying "talent will out" still holds true.

Horror Writers of America

Finally, I'd like to tell you about an organization that could become a very important part of your career.

Horror Writers of America (HWA) was formed a few years ago to establish a sense of community among those with a special interest in dark fantasy, horror, and occult fiction. They issue a regular newsletter, pass out annual awards, and provide up-to-date market information.

There are two levels of membership: Affiliate and Active. Affiliate members receive all the publications and services of Active members, including the right to recommend books and stories for the annual Bram Stoker Awards. Affiliate members are not, however, allowed to vote on these awards or in the election of HWA officers.

To qualify as an Active member, you must have sold three pieces of short fiction or articles related to the dark fantasy/horror/occult genre, none less than 2,500 words in length, at professional rates—at least three cents per word—or one book-length manuscript at an advance of no less than $2,000. You will also qualify for Active membership if you have sold one theatrical film or one ninety-minute TV movie or two thirty-minute episodic teleplays *that have been produced and either released in theaters or aired on nationwide television*, and for which you were paid the current Writer's Guild minimum.

If you wish to join, you may send a check, payable to Horror Writers of America, in the amount of $40 ($45 overseas) for the year (January through December). After July 1, annual dues will be prorated as follows:

July-September: $25 ($30 overseas)
October-December: $15 ($20 overseas)
Send your check to:

Horror Writers of America
Lisa Cantrell, Secretary
P.O. Box 655
Madison, NC 27025

And good luck with your sales!

13.
THE UNDEAD

When you are poised to enter any commercial field of endeavor — whether it be retail sales or brain surgery or horror writing — it is all too easy to believe that the established professionals in the field are godlike, superior beings with whom you share nothing in common, and that you are unworthy to join their exalted ranks.

Surely, you tell yourself, all the top horror writers have had far richer and more focused backgrounds than yours; they were probably child prodigies, had better educations, and began selling the moment they sent out their first manuscripts.

The reason for this chapter is to dispel such self-doubts. To show you that the purveyors of modern horror, the major writers of today, the authors whose novels regularly appear on national best-seller lists, come from backgrounds not unlike your own, that they faced the same obstacles to success and engaged in the same struggle to write and sell that you are undergoing. Their success can inspire yours — in the solid American tradition of: "If they can do it, so can I!"

Take the case of Stephen Edwin King . . .

Stephen King

More than twenty published books — critical studies, media histories, interviews, bibliographies, collected essays — have covered every aspect of the life and works of Stephen King, attesting to the immense popularity of this modern titan of terror. No other writer in history has approached King's incredible sales record around the globe, and his rags-to-riches saga is fascinating and instructive.

Born in Portland, Maine, of Scotch-Irish ancestry in September of 1947, his arrival was a surprise to Nellie King; she'd been told she would not be bearing children and had already adopted a baby, David, who became Steve's older brother.

Family life was unstable. When Steve was two, his parents separated; he never saw his father again. His mother raised him as a Methodist, and King remembers attending Bible school each week.

At six, he saw his first fright movie, *The Creature From the Black Lagoon*, launching a lifelong passion for the horror genre. Illness confined him to bed for most of his seventh year, and to pass the time, he began writing. At twelve, he discovered the work of H.P. Lovecraft and began submitting stories in 1959 to *The Magazine of Fantasy and Science Fiction*. It took him eight more years to make his first sale.

King began writing novels as a teenager in high school. He was attending the University of Maine, at Orono, when he sold his first horror tale to *Startling Mystery Stories*. In 1970, after graduating with a degree in English, he sought a teaching job. No luck. Steve went to work in an industrial laundry.

The next year, he married Tabitha Spruce and finally obtained a job teaching high school English at Hampton Academy. The Kings had their first child at the end of 1971.

By the winter of 1972, as Stephen King reached his midtwenties, the family was at a low point. He had written five novels but had been unable to place any of them. He had been selling a few of his short stories to *Cavalier*, but the checks were small, and even when they were added to his modest salary as a teacher, they failed to meet the family's financial needs. (The Kings now had a second child.)

They were living in a cramped trailer. The phone had been disconnected because they couldn't make the payments; their used car was in danger of being repossessed. Steve was drinking heavily, feeling that perhaps his dream of making a living from fiction was just that — a dream.

He was certain that his latest story, about a high school girl with special gifts, was a failure. He ripped the manuscript apart and tossed the pieces into a wastebasket. His wife dug it out, taped the torn pieces together, and said she *liked* the story. But it needed to be longer, she told him; the character of the teenager should be developed. In desperation, Steve turned it into a short novel, which he called *Carrie*. In the spring of 1973, Doubleday bought it for a $2,500 advance and printed the book a year later in hardcover. (Steve's mother died of cancer before the book's publication.)

Despite this first hardcover sale, things had not improved with the Kings; the bills were still pressing in relentlessly. Then Steve received news that paperback rights had been acquired by New American Library. He couldn't believe the price they were paying: NAL had advanced $400,000 for *Carrie*!

King immediately quit his teaching job and became a full-time writer.

With the success of *Carrie* as a hot movie in 1976 and the publication of his vampire novel, *'Salem's Lot*, Stephen King was off and running. And he never slowed down. In his first decade as a professional, his books sold fifty million copies. He became America's hottest writer, and in just fifteen years turned out twenty novels, five collections of short stories and novellas, a book-length personalized study of the horror genre, and a host of magazine pieces. Plus several screenplays.

When a new King book is published today, it automatically jumps to the top of best-seller lists and remains there for several months. The same is true with his paperbacks.

What kind of man is this King of horror?

A tall (6'4"), shambling, generally affable bear of a fellow, father of three children, bearded in winter, clean-shaven in summer, prone to wearing wrinkled jeans, scuffed boots, and T-shirts with weird slogans, he enjoys playing tennis and baseball, swimming, long walks in the woods of Maine, loud rock 'n' roll, and canned beer in six-packs. He's moody, gets severe headaches, and admits he's still afraid of the dark. He writes every day of the year (except Christmas, the Fourth of July, and his birthday). King owns two homes, both in Maine: a summer house in Center Lovell, on Kezar Lake, and a Victorian mansion in Bangor.

A private man, Steve dislikes being in the public eye but is friendly when cornered by fans. (I saw him sign so many books at a World Fantasy Convention that he had to soak his swollen hand in ice water; the line awaiting his signature stretched around the block.)

Anyone who reads horror knows his books — from the collections *Night Shift* and *Skeleton Crew* to the novels: *The Shining, The Dead Zone, Pet Sematary, It, Misery, The Tommyknockers, The Dark Half* . . . et al.

He now earns (including film money and overseas sales) approximately fifteen million dollars per book, and he publishes a new one every six months. That's thirty million a year, more than any writer in history.

Yes, as Stephen King keeps proving, there *is* big money in horror.

There are other writers currently working in this genre who deserve attention in terms of biographical perspective, each of them an expert in the literature of fear.

Let's start with a woman . . .

Anne Rice

Anne Rice lived in San Francisco for the past three decades, but has now returned to her roots in New Orleans. Her home is an 1859 townhouse, located in the same neighborhood where she was raised. There, with Stan Rice, her poet-painter husband, and a young son, she turns out best sellers about vampires and mummies. (She also writes erotica as "A.N. Roquelaure.")

Born in 1941, she and her three sisters were raised Roman Catholic. An early reader, she sought out Victorian horror books from the local library. When Anne was fourteen, her mother died; the family moved to Texas, where she attended high school and met her future husband. She earned an M.A. in creative writing at San Francisco State University in 1972, and married Stan Rice (who became a teacher at the university). She was determined to succeed as a novelist, but told her friends that writing was a therapeutic exercise. Inwardly, Anne envisioned herself as a major success, but as yet had no way to realize this vision.

In the early 1970s, she turned to an idea she'd had in 1960, a short story concerning an interview with a vampire. The story quickly turned into a novel. Anne submitted the manuscript to a writing contest, but it was thrown out of competition. She next took it to a writer's conference, where an agent read it and agreed to submit the novel to Knopf. It sold there and was published in 1976.

Interview With the Vampire reflected her Southern religious background (plus intensive period research). It concerns Louis, a creature of the night who catalogs his life and loves over two centuries, detailing murders, incest, seduction, and the myths of vampirism. A rich brew — followed by two bestselling sequel novels, *The Vampire Lestat* (1985) and *The Queen of the Damned* (1988).

In 1989, Rice's novel *The Mummy* signified the start of a new series. She's currently at work on a novel about a family of witches in modern New Orleans.

Anne Rice has always believed in herself; she knew she would be able to overcome rejection and tragedy (her first child died of leukemia in 1972) and achieve her inner goals.

For the author from New Orleans, success is no surprise.

James Herbert

James Herbert is Britain's bestselling writer of horror fiction. His first book, *The Rats*, which was published in 1974, shocked British readers with its graphic violence—yet the real-life background that inspired the novel was, according to Herbert, equally as horrific.

He was born in 1943 in London's impoverished East End, the third son of street vendors. His father, a hard-living brawler, sold fruit and vegetables in this depressed slum area. Young Herbert lived in Whitechapel, the killing ground of Jack the Ripper, in a condemned house overrun with rats.

He wanted to be a commercial artist, and as a teenager attended the Hornsey College of Art. Out of school, he worked as a paste-up man for a small art firm, then joined a London ad agency.

But James Herbert found that art was not his real vocation. He'd discovered American horror comics as a boy, and his imagination, fired by the real-life horrors of his childhood, led him to write *The Rats* when he was twenty-eight.

Despising the poverty of his youth, he has literally written his way to riches. He now owns a spacious country house in Sussex, drives a new Jaguar sedan, and enjoys a huge readership in Britain. His books—novels such as *The Fog*, *The Survivors*, *Shrine*, *The Dark*, and *Moon*, are also popular in the United States.

Herbert writes out all of his fiction by hand, feeling that the connection from brain to arm to fingers lends energy and immediacy to his work.

For James Herbert, each new novel is a fresh extension of his basic theme—that one individual, with talent and courage, *can* beat the system.

Peter Straub

Peter Straub looks like a New York banker. Bald, solemn (in photos), bespectacled, often in tie and business suit, he projects a sober-sided personality—yet claims that inside he's a wild man. The banker's facade hides a mind spilling over with fantastic images and bizarre plot ideas.

Straub's genre novels have all been major works, stylistically master-ful—from *Ghost Story* (1979) through *The Talisman* (with King, 1984). His works reflect subtle craftsmanship and superb imagery.

Born in Milwaukee in March 1943, he is one of three boys in the family. Peter recalls a strict Lutheran upbringing, which he ultimately rejected, and a father who was both violent and highly imaginative.

At seven, Peter was struck down by a car. During the long months of his recuperation, as he was attended at home by his mother (a professional nurse), he became a voracious reader, sparking a lifelong addiction.

Four years later, he joyfully discovered the landmark anthology, *Great Tales of Terror and the Supernatural*, and considers this an emotional entry point into the genre that he would later help revolutionize.

At sixteen, Peter Straub knew he wanted to be a novelist, although in practical terms, he felt that a more secure career was in order. He therefore set out to be a physician, but soon switched his major to English, obtaining a B.A. at the University of Wisconsin at Madison in 1965. He went on to collect his master's degree in contemporary literature at Columbia University, returning to Milwaukee as an English teacher.

After three years of teaching, he became bored, and by 1969, he was in Ireland, attending University College, Dublin. He finally decided that for-mal education was not the answer to his creative impulses. Straub set aside his doctoral dissertation on D.H. Lawrence to write (and sell) his first novel, the mainstream, nonhorror *Marriages*, published in 1973. After that, the die was cast: he became a full-time professional writer.

With his wife, Sally (they were married in 1966), Straub moved to Lon-don, spending two years on his second mainstream novel—which was rejected. In frustration, he turned to the horror field. He wrote two elegant genre novels, *Julia*, and *If You Could See Me Now*, both of which sold. He'd found his niche.

In 1977, while living in London, Straub met Stephen King, who would quickly become a primary influence in his life. Their friendship was in-stant and binding.

During this period, Straub wrote his first breakthrough novel, *Ghost Story*, and when the book was published in 1979, it jumped aboard best-seller lists. Universal Pictures optioned it for film. Straub achieved over-night prominence.

That same year, Peter and his family (he and his wife now had two children) returned to the United States after a decade in Europe. They found a rambling Victorian house in Westport, Connecticut, where Straub settled in to ply his craft.

Ghost Story became a hit on the big screen, and Straub's first genre novel was filmed in England as *The Haunting of Julia*, a dark and subtle excursion into terror.

Two more bestselling novels followed: *Shadowland* in 1980 and *Floating Dragon* in 1983; then it was Straub and King as a team, turning out *The Talisman* in 1984.

Peter now lives in a Manhattan apartment, writing each day to the loud beat of jazz over the speakers in his study. His latest novel, *Mystery*, was published in 1989, and there will be many more to come. Straub sees horror fiction as a well from which he can draw forth story after story.

He's certain the well will never run dry.

Dean R. Koontz

Writers who are able to command million-plus advances are still rare birds in the horror genre. **Dean R. Koontz** qualifies in this heady category. Beyond his ample talent, he has earned his high place by extremely hard work and staggering productivity. Koontz turns out novels with machine-gun rapidity and each of them seems better than the one that preceded it.

Under his own name and at least eight pseudonyms, he's written more than sixty books, working an eleven-hour day, six to seven days each week. He favors one-word titles—*Darkfall, Lightning, Phantoms, Whispers, Strangers, Midnight*—and wrote nineteen science-fiction novels before turning to the horror genre.

Dean's father was an alcoholic who was unable to hold a job, and the Koontz family experienced severe financial hardship as Dean grew up in Everett, Pennsylvania, where Koontz was born in July 1945.

After earning a degree in English, he became a high school teacher in his home state and was also active in a government poverty program.

He sold his first short story at the age of twenty when he was still a college student; he was married that same year. Dean needed money, and science fiction was an open market. In 1967, he began turning out science fiction novels at the rate of three a year. One of them, *Demon Seed*, was filmed by MGM. He left science fiction in the 1970s to concentrate on shock-suspense novels, making his breakthrough in 1980 with *Whispers*. Three years later, he created a classic in fright, *Phantoms*, and the horror field quickly claimed him as its own. (Koontz has also been prolific in the mystery genre, but even these books contain horrific elements.)

In 1981, he shared some of his hard-won knowledge with readers in *How to Write Best Selling Fiction*, and followed up this book with a perceptive chapter in *How to Write Tales of Horror, Fantasy, & Science Fiction* (Writer's Digest Books, 1987).

Dean Koontz has a wacky, surreal sense of humor, but he can deliver sheer terror on a page with the best in the business. And his stories resonate with life; readers identify with the characters he creates.

He lives and works in Orange, California, and his staggering financial success has had no slowdown effect on his prodigious output. Dean Koontz is an admitted word workaholic—perhaps in unconscious rebellion against an alcoholic father who could never hold a job.

Robert R. McCammon

Among recent horror writers who are building increasingly larger audiences is a Southern word wizard from Birmingham, Alabama—**Robert R. McCammon**.

Rick (as he likes to be called) jumped from paperback originals to hardcovers, then back to paperbacks before he made his major breakthrough.

The paperback original versus the hardcover represents an ongoing problem for authors. If a book is published first in a hardcover edition, it will generate far more reviews and rate much wider critical attention—but there's a catch. When softcover rights are sold, the hardcover house takes 50 percent of the paperback money. An author can usually earn more by going directly for a paperback original publication, yet in this version, a book receives practically no reviews and little or no critical attention; in addition, a paperback original reaches far fewer libraries.

McCammon's first four novels were paperback originals: *Baal, Night Boat, They Thirst,* and *Bethany's Sin*. He then switched to hardcover for *Mystery Walk* and *Usher's Passing,* but he was unhappy with the financial results. So he returned to selling his books as paperback originals, achieving the mass readership he desired with *Swan Song* in 1987. His next paperback, *Stinger*, did equally well—and he was finally among the top-selling names in the genre.

Born in Birmingham in July 1952, Rick McCammon was exposed to creativity from the outset, since his father was an accomplished musician. He obtained his B.A. from the University of Alabama in 1974. He went into advertising, working for the B. Dalton book chain in 1976. He then became copyeditor on the Birmingham *Post-Herald*. Fiction was a natural progression for him, and horror was the field he embraced in his first novel in 1978.

Rick and his wife, Sally (born and bred in the South), still live in Birmingham. After the television success of his story "Nightcrawlers," he was asked to work as a scriptwriter in Hollywood, but McCammon firmly refused the offer. He'll stay in the South, thank you, doing what he does best—bringing horror to the printed page.

The Awesome Power of Imagination

These brief bio portraits should encourage you. Several of the writers I've told you about overcame difficult childhoods, severe financial problems, and other major setbacks to achieve their career goals.

In the 1990s, the horror field remains very much alive and active. And the subject matter is widely varied. I recently selected two dozen horror novels at random and examined their contents. I found that these books dealt with remote islands, deadly winds, cults and curses, demons and devils, vampires, zombies, werewolves, giant rats, living skulls, psychic powers, angels of death, haunted relics, homicidal children, black magic, ancient evil, mysterious houses, and unearthly terrors.

As you can see, in horror, almost anything goes—and although new writers are constantly being warned about using evil children or haunted houses in their novels, editors still seem to be buying them. My theory is that while many subjects in horror have indeed been overworked, fresh variations on them will still sell to an editor. You need to find a new approach with surprising twists and gripping characters.

Until Robert Aickman came along in the 1950s, every possible version of the British ghost story had been written, and most editors believed this genre was creatively exhausted. Aickman didn't agree. He boldly and brilliantly produced his own special kind of ghosts, and in so doing promptly revitalized the genre.

So if you are really intent on writing about haunted houses or evil children or night-stalking vampires, don't let anyone discourage you. The most overworked clichés in horror can be given new life through your imagination. Always remember, of the five billion people on this planet, you are unique. No one else has your brain, your memories, your particular enthusiasms, your areas of knowledge, or your approach to living. Just as each snowflake is different, each person is different. But snowflakes can't write horror fiction. You can.

You have within your mind a unique, one-of-a-kind vision: put it to creative use by taking the elements of this genre and giving them your own twist. Make them *yours*. Reach inside yourself and find ways to make the old new again. It can be done, believe me.

Go for it!

Appendix

I — Horror Anthologies

II — Reference Books

Note: I have not attempted to include a checklist of novels in this Appendix. Most of the authors I have cited in the anthology listing have written excellent horror novels; it's worth your while to seek them out.

I. Horror Anthologies

I am providing here a key listing of more than fifty genre anthologies, arranged chronologically. Many of these books are out of print but can be obtained from libraries or booksellers. Others are available in paperback reprint.

The earliest anthologies in the genre date from the mid-1920s and were published in Great Britain—titles such as the *Not at Night* series (1925-1936), *The Ghost Book* (1926), *The Black Cap* (1928), and *Shudders* (1929). By the 1930s, horror tales began to be anthologized in the United States.

Creeps by Night: Chills and Thrills
Edited by Dashiell Hammett. New York: Day, 1931. Included: William Faulkner, John Collier, Conrad Aiken, H.P. Lovecraft, Stephen Vincent Benét, and Frank Belknap Long. An important breakthrough volume.

They Walk Again: An Anthology of Ghost Stories
Edited by Colin De La Mare. New York: Dutton, 1931. Included: Algernon Blackwood, Lord Dunsany, Ambrose Bierce, William Hope Hodgson, M.R. James, Walter de la Mare, W.W. Jacobs.

The Other Worlds: 25 Modern Stories of Mystery and Imagination
Edited by Phil Strong. New York: Funk, 1941. Included: Theodore Sturgeon, Lovecraft, Manly Wade Wellman, Seabury Quinn, August Derleth, Henry Kuttner.

The Midnight Reader: Great Stories of Haunting and Horror
Edited by Philip Van Doren Stern. New York: Holt, 1942. Included: Oliver Onions, M.R. James, Hugh Walpole, Blackwood, W.F. Harvey, Rudyard Kipling, J. Sheridan Le Fanu, Edgar Allan Poe, Alexander Woolcott. *Note:* For the softcover edition, in 1947, Pocket Books changed the title to: *The Pocket Book of Ghost Stories.*

The Moonlight Traveler: Great Tales of Fantasy and Imagination
Edited by Philip Van Doren Stern. New York: Doubleday, 1943. Included: H.G. Wells, Robert Louis Stevenson, A.E. Coppard, Somerset Maugham, Dunsany, Aiken, Poe, Kipling, Saki.

Tales of Terror
Edited by Boris Karloff. New York: World, 1943. Included: Bram Stoker, Bierce, Hugh Walpole, Robert Hugh Benson, Faulkner, Poe, Harvey, Blackwood, Onions. My introduction to horror, and still a marvelous collection.

Great Tales of Terror and the Supernatural
Edited by Herbert A. Wise and Phyllis Fraser. New York: Random House, 1944. Included: Poe, Wilkie Collins, Bierce, Jacobs, Wells, Saki, Aiken, Faulkner, Collier, Nathaniel Hawthorne, Charles Dickens, Le Fanu, Fitz-James O'Brien, Henry James, Guy de Maupassant, M.R. James, Arthur Machen, Kipling, Edward Lucas White, Blackwood, Onions, Coppard, Isak Dinesen, Lovecraft. The first classic anthology in the genre; a key volume for the enthusiast. A massive 1,080 pages.

Pause to Wonder: Stories of the Marvelous, Mysterious, and Strange
Edited by Marjorie Fischer and Rolfe Humphries. New York: Julian Messner, 1944. Included: William Butler Yeats, de la Mare, Machen, G.K. Chesterton, Oscar Wilde, Jacobs, Henry James, D.H. Lawrence, Collier, Maugham, Wells.

Sleep No More: Twenty Masterpieces of Horror for the Connoisseur
Edited by August Derleth. New York: Murray Hill, 1944. Included: M. R. James, Blackwood, Clark Ashton Smith, H. Russell Wakefield,

Collier, Robert Bloch, M.P. Shiel, Carl Jacobi, Robert Chambers, Robert E. Howard, Long, Lovecraft. The first of several important genre anthologies from the founder of Arkham House.

And the Darkness Falls: Masterpieces of Horror and the Supernatural
Edited by Boris Karloff. New York: World, 1946. Included: Onions, Benson, Bierce, Arthur Conan Doyle, Blackwood, Derleth, Henry R. Wakefield, Maugham, Collier, Yeats, Poe, Cornell Woolrich (as William Irish), de la Mare, Jacobs, Dunsany, Smith, Hugh Walpole, Conrad, Lovecraft. Karloff's second anthology is superb, a classic collection.

Strange and Fantastic Stories: Fifty Tales of Terror, Horror and Fantasy
Edited by Joseph A. Margolies. New York: McGraw-Hill, 1946. Included: Benét, Benson, Hawthorne, Dickens, Bierce, Blackwood, Harvey, Collier, Conrad, Woolcott, Henry James, Kipling, Lawrence, Le Fanu, Stevenson, Wells, O'Brien, Machen.

Who Knocks? Twenty Masterpieces of the Spectral for the Connoisseur
Edited by August Derleth. New York: Rinehart, 1946. Included: Ray Bradbury (his first book appearance), Blackwood, Coppard, Lovecraft, Wakefield, Harvey, Sturgeon, Quinn, Edward Lucas White, Benson, Le Fanu.

Timeless Stories for Today and Tomorrow
Edited by Ray Bradbury. New York: Bantam, 1952. Included: Kuttner, Shirley Jackson, Nigel Kneale, Roald Dahl, William Sansom, John Cheever, Franz Kafka. The first of Bradbury's two genre anthologies. A paperback original.

The Supernatural Reader
Edited by Groff and Lucy Conklin. New York: Lippincott, 1953. Included: Bradbury, Coppard, Sturgeon, O'Brien, Kneale, Collier, M.R. James, Dunsany, Bierce.

Science Fiction Terror Tales
Edited by Groff Conklin. New York: Gnome Press, 1955. Included: Bradbury, Fredric Brown, Richard Matheson, Sturgeon, Anthony Boucher, Philip K. Dick.

The Circus of Dr. Lao . . . and Other Improbable Stories
Edited by Ray Bradbury. New York: Bantam, 1956. Included: Kneale, Dahl, Jackson, Hawthorne, Kuttner. A paperback original.

S-F: The Year's Greatest Science-Fiction and Fantasy
Edited by Judith Merril. New York: Dell, 1956. *Note:* The first of a dozen (into 1969) volumes edited by Merril in this series, which mixed SF with horror and fantasy. Most of the books were titled *The Year's Best S-F*, the last simply *SF-12*. The volumes included all of the major writers and many newcomers.

The Fiend in You
Edited by Charles Beaumont (and William F. Nolan, anon.) New York: Ballantine, 1962. Included: Matheson, Beaumont, Nolan, Bloch, Bradbury, Fritz Leiber. A paperback original.

The Playboy Book of Horror and the Supernatural
Edited "by the Editors of Playboy" (actually, Ray Russell). Chicago: Playboy Press, 1967. Included: Beaumont, Bradbury, Nolan, Russell, Matheson, Collier, Brown, Bloch, Jack Finney.

The Year's Best Horror Stories
Edited by Gerald Page. New York: DAW, 1971. *Note:* This was the first in the ongoing series now edited by Karl Edward Wagner. Thus far, nineteen volumes have been published; Page edited the earlier ones. These volumes have included all of the major contemporary writers from King to Etchison. They are paperback originals.

The Hollywood Nightmare: Tales of Fantasy and Horror from the Film World
Edited by Peter Haining. New York: Taplinger, 1971. Included: Bloch, Derleth, Nolan, Kuttner, Bradbury, Russell, Leiber, Beaumont, Collier, J.G. Ballard.

The Lucifer Society: Macabre Tales by Great Modern Writers
Edited by Peter Haining. New York: New American Library, 1972. Included: Maugham, Faulkner, Truman Capote, Chesterton, J. B. Priestley. A paperback original.

Frights: New Stories of Suspense and Supernatural Terror
Edited by Kirby McCauley. New York: St. Martin's Press, 1976. Included: Dennis Etchison, Leiber, Russell Kirk, Brian Lumley, Davis Grubb, Robert Aickman, Nolan, Bloch, Ramsey Campbell. An influential anthology.

Whispers: An Anthology of Fantasy and Horror
Edited by Stuart David Schiff. New York: Doubleday, 1977. *Note:* This was the first of six volumes under this title (into 1987). They mixed new fiction with reprints from *Whispers* magazine and included the best of modern writers in the genre. A Schiff-edited volume, *The Best of Whispers*, is forthcoming.

Strangeness: A Collection of Strikingly Uncommon Fiction
Edited by Thomas M. Disch and Charles Naylor. New York: Scribners, 1977. Included: Jackson, Joyce Carol Oates, Thomas Disch, Sansom.

Shadows
Edited by Charles L. Grant. New York: Doubleday, 1978. *Note:* This was the first of eleven volumes under this title (into 1990). Included are the best of the modern genre. Its editor coined the term *Dark Fantasy*.

Nightmares
Edited by Charles L. Grant. Chicago: Playboy Press, 1979. Included: Stephen King, Etchison, Chelsea Quinn Yarbro, Jack Dann, Richard Christian Matheson, Russell, Campbell, Nolan. A paperback original.

Dark Forces: New Stories of Suspense and Supernatural Horror
Edited by Kirby McCauley. New York: Viking Press, 1980. Included: King (short novel), Etchison, Oates, T.E.D. Klein, Bradbury, Bloch, Edward Bryant, Grubb, Aickman, Wagner, Gene Wolfe, Sturgeon, Campbell, Kirk, Lisa Tuttle, Grant, Wellman, Richard Matheson, and Richard Christian Matheson. A classic anthology of modern horror.

Horrors
Edited by Charles L. Grant. New York: Playboy, 1981. Included: King, Yarbro, Nolan, Etchison, Tuttle, Dann, Steve Rasnic Tem, David Morrell. A paperback original.

The Arbor House Treasury of Horror and the Supernatural
Edited by Bill Pronzini, Barry Malzberg, and Martin H. Greenberg. New York: Arbor House, 1981. Included: (under the title "Grandmasters") Poe, Hawthorne, Le Fanu, Stoker, Henry James, Wells, Bierce, Lovecraft, Bloch, Woolrich, Faulkner, Sturgeon, Leiber, Capote, Brown; (under the title "Modern Masters") Wagner, Russell, Disch, Campbell, King, Dann, Oates, Grant, Nolan. Landmark anthology at 600 pages,

covering the entire genre, classic to modern. *Note:* Reissued under the title *Great Tales of Horror and the Supernatural.*

Modern Masters of Horror
Edited by Frank Coffey. New York: Coward, McCann & Geoghegan, 1981. Included: King, John Coyne, Bloch, Campbell, Gary Brandner, Robert R. McCammon, Nolan, Grubb, Richard Laymon, Graham Masterton.

The Arbor House Celebrity Book of Horror Stories
Edited by Charles G. Waugh and Martin H. Greenberg. New York: Arbor House, 1982. Included: M.R. James, Bloch, White, Jacobs, Bradbury, King, Cheever, Brown, Ira Levin, Campbell, Matheson, Nolan, Tuttle, Oates, Henry James, Poe, A. Merritt, Lovecraft. A unique idea, having celebrities choose favorite horror stories and introducing their choices.

Fears
Edited by Charles L. Grant. New York: Berkley, 1983. Included: Yarbro, Dann, Nolan, Morrell, Etchison, Al Sarrantonio, Joe R. Lansdale, George R.R. Martin. A paperback original.

The Dodd, Mead Gallery of Horror: Twenty Portraits in Terror by Modern Masters
Edited by Charles L. Grant. New York: Dodd, Mead, 1983. Included: Nolan, Joseph Payne Brennan, Alan Ryan, Bloch, Klein, Campbell, Dann, Coyne, Etchison, Morrell, Tem, Yarbro, Sturgeon, King.

Masques: All-New Works of Horror and the Supernatural
Edited by J.N. Williamson. Baltimore: Maclay, 1984. *Note:* An ongoing series of volumes—*Masques II* was published in 1987, *Masques III*, in 1989—that includes all the best modern horror authors. St. Martin's Press published the third volume.

Masterpieces of Terror and the Supernatural: A Treasury of Spellbinding Tales Old and New
Edited by Marvin Kaye. New York: Doubleday, 1985. Included: Stoker, Sturgeon, Stevenson, Le Fanu, Poe, Russell, Matheson, Merritt, Jack London, Bierce, Tennessee Williams, Aickman, Hawthorne, Bloch, O'Brien, Lovecraft. A potent collection; 623 pages.

Midnight
Edited by Charles L. Grant. New York: TOR, 1985. Included: Campbell, Brennan, Bloch, Nolan. A paperback original.

A Treasury of American Horror Stories: 51 Spine-Chilling Tales from Every State in the Union, plus Washington, D.C.
Edited by Frank D. McSherry, Jr., Charles G. Waugh, and Martin H. Greenberg. New York: Bonanza, 1985. Included: Bierce, Matheson, London, Bloch, Stevenson, Lovecraft, Jacobi, Nolan, King, Benét, Wellman, Grubb, Ardath Mayhar, Whitley Strieber, Derleth. Unique idea: a story set in each state. Massive at 670 pages.

Nukes: Four Horror Writers on the Ultimate Horror
Edited by John Maclay. Baltimore: Maclay, 1986. Included: Mort Castle, Lansdale, J.N. Williamson, Jessica A. Salmonson. A paperback original treating the subject of atomic disaster.

Masters of Darkness
Edited by Dennis Etchison. New York: TOR, 1986. *Note:* A three-volume set of stories chosen by their authors; *Masters of Darkness II* was published in 1988, *Masters of Darkness III*, in 1990. The major authors of today are included: King, Campbell, Matheson, Wagner, Yarbro, Nolan, Tem, R.C. Matheson, Tuttle, Thomas F. Monteleone, Martin. Paperback original. A forthcoming hardcover will incorporate all three volumes under one cover.

Cutting Edge
Edited by Dennis Etchison. New York: Doubleday, 1986. Included: Peter Straub, Wagner, Roberta Lannes, Grant, Tem, Les Daniels, R.C. Matheson, Yarbro, Nolan, Campbell, Russell, Clive Barker, Bloch, Bryant, Strieber. Another modern landmark anthology.

Tales of the Dead
Edited by Bill Pronzini. New York: Bonanza, 1986. *Note:* Includes the full contents of three earlier genre anthologies edited by Pronzini; *Voodoo!*, *Mummy!*, and *Ghoul!*. Contains a bibliography of genre material relating to each category.

Black Wine
Edited by Douglas E. Winter. Niles, IL: Dark Harvest, 1986. Included: six stories each by Campbell and Grant. *Note:* Dark Harvest has pub-

lished a number of recent anthologies (various editors), collecting new work by three authors in each volume, under the overall title *Night Visions*.

The Dark Descent
Edited by David G. Hartwell. New York: TOR, 1987. Included: Le Fanu, Poe, Bierce, M.R. James, Lovecraft, Faulkner, Leiber, Bloch, Collier, Jackson, Oates, Bradbury, King, Barker, Etchison. A major work. An overview of the genre from classic to modern. Massive at 1,011 pages.

The Year's Best Fantasy
Edited by Ellen Datlow and Terri Windling. New York: St. Martin's Press, 1988. *Note:* This is an ongoing annual series and includes a summation of fantasy by Windling and a summation of horror by Datlow. Edward Bryant covers horror and fantasy on the screen. An important series.

Prime Evil: New Stories by the Masters of Modern Horror
Edited by Douglas E. Winter. New York: New American Library, 1988. Included: Straub, Barker, King, Morrell, Campbell, Strieber, Thomas Tessier, Etchison, Grant.

The Best of Masques
Edited by J.N. Williamson. New York: Berkley, 1988. Included: McCammon, Matheson, F. Paul Wilson, Campbell, Bloch, Nolan, Tem, Bradbury, Monteleone, Grant, Russell, Williamson, Lansdale, King, Etchison, R.C. Matheson. Selected from the first two volumes in this series. A paperback original.

Weird Tales: 32 Unearthed Terrors
Edited by Stefan Dziemianowicz, Robert Weinberg, and Martin H. Greenberg. New York: Bonanza, 1988. Reprints a story from each year of the classic horror magazine. Included are all of the major authors who wrote for *Weird Tales*.

The Best of Shadows
Edited by Charles L. Grant. New York: Doubleday, 1988. Included: Sarrantonio, Yarbro, Morrell, Ryan, Campbell, Tem, Tuttle. Grant's best, selected from the first ten volumes of this series. With a listing of all ninety-three authors whose work appeared in volumes 1-10 and their stories.

131

Scare Care
Edited by Graham Masterton. New York: TOR, 1989. Included: Campbell, Nolan, William Relling, J.N. Williamson, Lumley, James Kisner, John Maclay, Dahl, Masterton, Grant, James Herbert, David R. Silva, Tem. *Note:* Edited for the Scare Care Trust, which provides money for abused and needy children.

Post Mortem: New Tales of Ghostly Horror
Edited by Paul F. Olson and David B. Silva. New York: St. Martin's Press, 1989. Included: Tessier, Campbell, Nolan, Brandner, Tem, Grant, Monteleone, Silva, McCammon, Dean R. Koontz.

Urban Horrors
Edited by William F. Nolan and Martin H. Greenberg. Niles, IL: Dark Harvest, 1990. Included: Etchison, Cheever, Jackson, Leiber, Richard Matheson, R.C. Matheson, Beaumont, J.N. Williamson, Lansdale, Maclay, Kisner, Nolan, Russell, Oates, Dick, Campbell.

For a listing of more than 150 fantasy and horror anthologies, with main titles and authors included, see Appendix II in *Who's Who in Horror and Fantasy Fiction*, by Mike Ashley (New York: Taplinger, 1978).

II. Reference Books

These twenty-seven volumes form an extensive cross-section; they involve the history of the genre in print and on film; works on Stephen King and Boris Karloff, on collecting, on the 100 "Best" books; essays on writing for the field; collected interviews; scripts; an examination of *The Twilight Zone*; and biographies of all the major horror writers.

They are arranged in descending chronological order, beginning in 1990.

Horror Literature: A Reader's Guide
Edited by Neil Barron. New York: Garland, 1990. Surveys and discussions of the development of, and current influences in, horror fiction. Survey dates from 1762-1988. Comprehensive and excellent. An all-in-one guide.

Dark Dreamers: Conversations with the Masters of Horror
By Stanley Wiater. New York: Avon, 1990. Interviews with King,

Straub, Bloch, J. N. Williamson, Campbell, Etchison, Koontz, Lansdale, Richard Matheson, McCammon, Morrell, Rice, Strieber, and others.

Horror: A Connoisseur's Guide to Literature and Film
By Leonard Wolf. New York: Facts on File, 1989. A fine bibliography of genre materials.

Bare Bones: Conversations on Terror with Stephen King
Edited by Tim Underwood and Chuck Miller. New York: McGraw-Hill, 1988. The collected interviews with the master of modern horror.

The Complete Guide to Standard Script Formats: Part I: The Screenplay
By Hillis R. Cole, Jr. and Judith R. Haag. North Hollywood: CMC Publishing, 1988. The essential guide to script formats, this book defines and explains the standards by which all entertainment industry scripts are judged. If a submitted script is not formatted properly (whether by a typing service or the writer), it will immediately be rejected as nonprofessional. Scripts (in contrast to prose) consist of units of time (seconds and minutes); therefore, standard industry formatting is necessary. If you're going to write a script, buy this book . . . then *use* it.

Horror: 100 Best Books
Edited by Stephen Jones and Kim Newman. New York: Carroll & Graf, 1988. A superb roundup of the finest works; each choice is introduced by an authority in the field.

How to Sell Your Screenplay: The Real Rules of Film and Television
By Carl Sautter. New York: New Chapter Press, 1988. An essential book for anyone who seriously wants to write for films or television. The only book I know of that explains how the entertainment industry *actually* operates. Contains the nitty-gritty information every beginning scripter needs to learn.

Plot
By Ansen Dibell. Cincinnati, OH: Writer's Digest Books, 1988. A solid and helpful guide to plotting, packed with information essential to the beginning novelist.

How to Write Tales of Horror, Fantasy, & Science Fiction
Edited by J.N. Williamson. Cincinnati, OH: Writer's Digest Books, 1987. Essays on genre fiction, leaning toward horror, with a massive

133

series of checklists. Included: Bradbury, Koontz, Bloch, Castle, Tem, Kisner, Mayhar, Grant, McCammon, Campbell, J.N. Williamson, R.C. Matheson, Wilson, Nolan. Instructive and rewarding.

Making a Good Script Great: A Guide for Writing and Rewriting
By Linda Seger. New York: Dodd, Mead & Co., 1987. An important book by an experienced Hollywood script consultant. Recommended.

Kingdom of Fear: The World of Stephen King
Edited by Tim Underwood and Chuck Miller. San Francisco: Underwood-Miller, 1986. A collection of critical essays on King's work. Included: Strieber, Barker, Nolan, McDowell, Campbell, Monteleone. Other collections of essays on King have been published, including the earlier *Fear Itself*, also from Underwood-Miller, but this collection best serves its subject.

The Penguin Encyclopedia of Horror and the Supernatural
Edited by Jack Sullivan. New York: Viking, 1986. Massive and all-inclusive, with biographical/critical coverage of the major world writers, plus essays on every aspect of the genre. Fully illustrated, large-sized. An absolute *must* — the essential work in the field to date.

Faces of Fear: Encounters with the Creators of Modern Horror
By Douglas E. Winter. New York: Berkley, 1985. Interviews with Bloch, Matheson, Blatty, Etchison, Campbell, Morrell, Herbert, Grant, Klein, Ryan, Coyne, Andrews, McDowell, Strieber, Barker, Straub, and King. With photos as well as listings of Winter's "bests" in horror fiction and films. Winter's interviews are incisive, informative, highly personal, and instructive. As the outstanding critic in the genre, Winter achieves depth and meaning in each profile. A major work in the field.

Supernatural Fiction Writers
Edited by Everett F. Bleiler. New York: Scribners, 1985. (Two volumes) Some 150 writers are extensively covered here, biographically and critically. In Volume 1: French and German writers, British Gothic and Romantic writers, British Victorian writers, and early twentieth-century British writers. In Volume 2: British postwar writers, American writers of the early nineteenth-century and the Victorian period, American writers of the early to middle twentieth-century, American pulp writers, plus modern writers, British and American. Amazingly comprehensive.

The key biographical work in the genre.

Stephen King: The Art of Darkness
By Douglas E. Winter. New York: New American Library, 1984. A biographical/critical study. With a full bibliography of King's work, including motion-picture and television adaptations. Extremely readable, based on interviews and extensive research. (Updated in paperback.) The standard work on this author.

The Guide to Supernatural Fiction
By Everett F. Bleiler. Kent, OH: Kent State University Press, 1983. Full descriptions of 1,775 books, from 1750 to 1960, including minidescriptions of many hundreds of short stories. Truly monumental. An amazing example of scholarship.

The Twilight Zone Companion
By Marc Scott Zicree. New York: Bantam, 1982. A comprehensive, episode-by-episode guide to Rod Serling's famed television show. Illustrated with photos from each episode; contains biographical portraits of Rod Serling, Charles Beaumont, Richard Matheson, and George Clayton Johnson — all major contributors to the series. Since *The Twilight Zone* was the most influential television show in the genre, this book is historically important. It's also great fun!

The Creature Features Movie Guide: An A to Z Encyclopedia to the Cinema of the Fantastic
By John Stanley. Pacifica, CA: Creatures at Large, 1981. This volume, covering the genre through 1980, contains 2,753 of Stanley's minireviews of motion-picture and television films. (Subsequent volumes are updated.) Brisk, clever, informative. A joy for film buffs.

Horror Literature: A Core Collection and Reference Guide
Edited by Marshall B. Tymn. New York: Bowker, 1981. Basically, this book consists of annotated checklists: "The Gothic Romance 1762-1820" (422 entries); "The Residual Gothic Impulse 1824-1873" (101 entries); "Psychological, Antiquarian, and Cosmic Horror 1872-1919" (260 entries); and "The Modern Masters 1920-1980" (311 entries). Also includes sections on "The Horror Pulps 1933-1940," "Supernatural Verse in English," and "Reference Sources." Another key volume in the genre.

The T.V. Scriptwriter's Handbook
 By Alfred Brenner. Cincinnati, OH: Writer's Digest Books, 1980. A
 good, basic guide.

Danse Macabre
 By Stephen King. New York: Everest House, 1979. A personal view of
 the genre, based on King's loves and hates. Casual, often funny, but
 written with a genuine passion for things horrific. And often overtly
 autobiographical. With a listing of his favorite films and books. Important and readable. *Note:* The definitive edition was published in paperback by Berkley in 1983, incorporating corrections and revisions.

Who's Who in Horror and Fantasy Fiction
 By Mike Ashley. New York: Taplinger, 1978. Includes brief entries on
 400 writers. Also contains a chronology of major books and stories in
 the genre from 2,000 B.C.E. through 1977, and appendices of books
 and stories (A to Z), weird fiction anthologies, and a list of 100 weird/
 horror fiction magazines, extending back to *Marvellous Magazine* in
 1802! A milestone in the field. Of major value.

Living in Fear: A History of Horror in the Mass Media
 By Les Daniels. New York: Scribners, 1975. The genre as it impacts on
 pop culture. Historically valuable.

Karloff: The Man, the Monster, the Movies
 By Denis Gifford. New York: Curtis Books, 1973. Karloff's life history,
 with a film-by-film rundown of his 157 motion pictures from 1919 into
 1968. (Karloff died in 1969 at age 81.) Plus listings of his other works.
 An essential guide to the greatest actor in horror, the legendary Frankenstein monster himself.

Val Lewton: The Reality of Terror
 By Joel E. Siegel. New York: Viking Press, 1973. A cinematic study of
 one of the genre's most influential producer-writers. With chapters on
 each of his major films, classics such as *The Body Snatcher, The Leop-
 ard Man, Cat People, I Walked With a Zombie, Isle of the Dead*, and
 Bedlam.

Focus on the Horror Film
 Edited by Roy Huss and T.J. Ross. Englewood Cliffs, NJ: Prentice-Hall,
 1972. Essays on horror films, from Gothic to psychological. Includes a

filmography, listing genre films from 1908 into 1971, worldwide. Also a bibliography. A rewarding overview.

An Illustrated History of the Horror Film
By Carlos Clarens. New York: Putnam, 1967. A full examination of the genre; casts and credits of the 300-plus films are examined in the main text. Photo-illustrated. This history-analysis is now dated, but retains importance as a study of the field into the 1960s. *Note:* Larry Edmunds Cinema Bookshop carries a full line of new and used books relating to horror in motion pictures and television, as well as all the books listed herein that relate to scripting. They deal by mail and may be addressed at: 6658 Hollywood Boulevard, Hollywood, CA 90028. Telephone: (213) 463-3273. A number of other specialty booksellers stock back titles of fiction and nonfiction volumes, as well as current works in the genre. Their prices vary, but each is reliable.

Weinberg Books, P.O. Box 423, Oak Forest, IL 60452
Night Winds Books, P.O. Box 28821, Kansas City, MO 64118
The Overlook Connection, P.O. Box 526, Woodstock, GA 30188
L.W. Curry, Elizabethtown, NY 12932
Pandora's, Ltd., Box 54, Neche, ND 58265 (This dealer carries a huge inventory of paperbacks and magazines.)

Index

Other Books of Interest

Annual Market Directories
Save 15% on the following
Writer's Digest Books Annual Directories!

Maximize your chances of selling your work with these market directories that offer up-to-date listings of markets for your books, articles, stories, novels, poems, gags, photos, designs, illustrations, and more. Each listing gives contact name and address, details on the type(s) of work they're seeking, pay/royalty rates, and submission requirements, to help you target your work to the best prospects.

Artist's Market, edited by Lauri Miller $22.95
Children's Writer's & Illustrator's Market, edited by Lisa Carpenter (paper) $17.95
Guide to Literary Agents & Art/Photo Reps, edited by Robin Gee $15.95
Humor & Cartoon Markets, edited by Bob Staake $18.95
Novel & Short Story Writer's Market, edited by Robin Gee (paper) $19.95
Photographer's Market, edited by Michael Willins $22.95
Poet's Market, by Michael J. Bugeja and Christine Martin $19.95
Songwriter's Market, edited by Michael Oxley $19.95
Writer's Market, edited by Mark Kissling $26.95

To receive your **15% discount** on any of the above listed Market Books, simply mention **#6299** when phoning in your order to toll-free **1-800-289-0963**.

General Writing Books
Beginning Writer's Answer Book, edited by Kirk Polking (paper) $13.95
Dare to Be a Great Writer, by Leonard Bishop (paper) $14.95
Discovering the Writer Within, by Bruce Ballenger & Barry Lane $17.95
Freeing Your Creativity, by Marshall Cook $17.95
Getting the Words Right: How to Rewrite, Edit and Revise, by Theodore A. Rees Cheney (paper) $12.95
How to Write a Book Proposal, by Michael Larsen (paper) $11.95
How to Write Fast While Writing Well, by David Fryxell $17.95
How to Write with the Skill of a Master and the Genius of a Child, by Marshall J. Cook $18.95
Just Open a Vein, edited by William Brohaugh $6.99
Knowing Where to Look: The Ultimate Guide to Research, by Lois Horowitz (paper) $18.95
Make Your Words Work, by Gary Provost $17.95
On Being a Writer, edited by Bill Strickland (paper) $16.95
Pinckert's Practical Grammar, by Robert C. Pinckert (paper) $11.95
12 Keys to Writing Books That Sell, by Kathleen Krull (paper) $12.95
The 28 Biggest Writing Blunders, by William Noble $12.95
The 29 Most Common Writing Mistakes & How to Avoid Them, by Judy Delton (paper) $9.95
The Wordwatcher's Guide to Good Writing & Grammar, by Morton S. Freeman (paper) $15.95
Word Processing Secrets for Writers, by Michael A. Banks & Ansen Dibell (paper) $14.95
The Writer's Book of Checklists, by Scott Edelstein $16.95
The Writer's Digest Guide to Manuscript Formats, by Buchman & Groves $18.95
The Writer's Essential Desk Reference, edited by Glenda Neff $19.95

Nonfiction Writing
The Complete Guide to Writing Biographies, by Ted Schwarz $6.99
Creative Conversations: The Writer's Guide to Conducting Interviews, by Michael Schumacher $16.95
How to Do Leaflets, Newsletters, & Newspapers, by Nancy Brigham (paper) $14.95
How to Write Irresistible Query Letters, by Lisa Collier Cool (paper) $10.95
The Writer's Digest Handbook of Magazine Article Writing, edited by Jean M. Fredette (paper) $11.95

Fiction Writing
The Art & Craft of Novel Writing, by Oakley Hall $17.95
Best Stories from New Writers, edited by Linda Sanders $5.99
Characters & Viewpoint, by Orson Scott Card $13.95
The Complete Guide to Writing Fiction, by Barnaby Conrad $18.95
Creating Characters: How to Build Story People, by Dwight V. Swain $16.95
Creating Short Fiction, by Damon Knight (paper) $10.95
Dialogue, by Lewis Turco $13.95
The Fiction Writer's Silent Partner, by Martin Roth $19.95
Get That Novel Started! (And Keep Going 'Til You Finish), by Donna Levin $17.95
Handbook of Short Story Writing: Vol. I, by Dickson and Smythe (paper) $12.95
Handbook of Short Story Writing: Vol. II, edited by Jean Fredette (paper) $12.95
How to Write & Sell Your First Novel, by Collier & Leighton (paper) $12.95
Manuscript Submission, by Scott Edelstein $13.95
Mastering Fiction Writing, by Kit Reed $18.95
Plot, by Ansen Dibell $13.95
Practical Tips for Writing Popular Fiction, by Robyn Carr $17.95
Spider Spin Me a Web: Lawrence Block on Writing Fiction, by Lawrence Block $16.95
Theme & Strategy, by Ronald B. Tobias $13.95

The 38 Most Common Writing Mistakes, by Jack M. Bickham $12.95
Writer's Digest Handbook of Novel Writing, $18.95
Writing the Novel: From Plot to Print, by Lawrence Block (paper) $11.95

Special Interest Writing Books

Armed & Dangerous: A Writer's Guide to Weapons, by Michael Newton (paper) $14.95
Cause of Death: A Writer's Guide to Death, Murder & Forensic Medicine, by Keith D. Wilson, M.D. $15.95
The Children's Picture Book: How to Write It, How to Sell It, by Ellen E.M. Roberts (paper) $19.95
Children's Writer's Word Book, by Alijandra Mogliner $19.95
Comedy Writing Secrets, by Mel Helitzer (paper) $15.95
The Complete Book of Feature Writing, by Leonard Witt $18.95
Creating Poetry, by John Drury $18.95
Deadly Doses: A Writer's Guide to Poisons, by Serita Deborah Stevens with Anne Klarner (paper) $16.95
Editing Your Newsletter, by Mark Beach (paper) $18.50
Families Writing, by Peter Stillman (paper) $12.95
A Guide to Travel Writing & Photography, by Ann & Carl Purcell (paper) $22.95
Hillary Waugh's Guide to Mysteries & Mystery Writing, by Hillary Waugh $19.95
How to Pitch & Sell Your TV Script, by David Silver $17.95
How to Write & Sell Greeting Cards, Bumper Stickers, T-Shirts and Other Fun Stuff, by Molly Wigand (paper) 15.95
How to Write & Sell True Crime, by Gary Provost $17.95
How to Write Horror Fiction, by William F. Nolan $15.95
How to Write Mysteries, by Shannon OCork $13.95
How to Write Romances, by Phyllis Taylor Pianka $15.95
How to Write Science Fiction & Fantasy, by Orson Scott Card $13.95
How to Write Tales of Horror, Fantasy & Science Fiction, edited by J.N. Williamson (paper) $12.95
How to Write the Story of Your Life, by Frank P. Thomas (paper) $11.95
How to Write Western Novels, by Matt Braun $1.00
The Magazine Article: How To Think It, Plan It, Write It, by Peter Jacobi $17.95
Mystery Writer's Handbook, by The Mystery Writers of America (paper) $11.95
The Poet's Handbook, by Judson Jerome (paper) $11.95
Powerful Business Writing, by Tom McKeown $12.95
Scene of the Crime: A Writer's Guide to Crime-Scene Investigation, by Anne Wingate, Ph.D. $15.95
Successful Scriptwriting, by Jurgen Wolff & Kerry Cox (paper) $14.95
The Writer's Complete Crime Reference Book, by Martin Roth $19.95
The Writer's Guide to Conquering the Magazine Market, by Connie Emerson $17.95
Writing for Children & Teenagers, 3rd Edition, by Lee Wyndham & Arnold Madison (paper) $12.95
Writing Mysteries: A Handbook by the Mystery Writers of America, Edited by Sue Grafton, $18.95
Writing the Modern Mystery, by Barbara Norville (paper) $12.95

The Writing Business

A Beginner's Guide to Getting Published, edited by Kirk Polking (paper) $11.95
Business & Legal Forms for Authors & Self-Publishers, by Tad Crawford (paper) $4.99
The Complete Guide to Self-Publishing, by Tom & Marilyn Ross (paper) $16.95
How to Write with a Collaborator, by Hal Bennett with Michael Larsen $1.00
How You Can Make $25,000 a Year Writing, by Nancy Edmonds Hanson (paper) $14.95
This Business of Writing, by Gregg Levoy $19.95
Writer's Guide to Self-Promotion & Publicity, by Elane Feldman $16.95
A Writer's Guide to Contract Negotiations, by Richard Balkin (paper) $4.25
Writing A to Z, edited by Kirk Polking $24.95

To order directly from the publisher, include $3.00 postage and handling for 1 book and $1.00 for each additional book. Allow 30 days for delivery.

Writer's Digest Books
1507 Dana Avenue, Cincinnati, Ohio 45207
Credit card orders call TOLL-FREE
1-800-289-0963
Stock is limited on some titles; prices subject to change without notice.

Write to this same address for information on *Writer's Digest* magazine, *Story* magazine, Writer's Digest Book Club, Writer's Digest School, and Writer's Digest Criticism Service.